LONG REINING

FROM THE BEGINNING
THROUGH THE LEVADE

Dr Thomas Ritter

LONG REINING
FROM THE BEGINNING
THROUGH THE LEVADE

While the author and the publishers have compiled
and reviewed the contents of this book with great care
and to the best of their knowledge and belief, no
liability can be accepted for any injury to humans or
animals or animals which might arise as a result of
actions and/ or decisions taken by the book`s readers

IMPRINT

Copyright © 2015 Cadmos Publishing Limited,
Richmond, UK
Copyright of original edition © 2014 Cadmos Verlag
GmbH, Schwarzenbek, Germany

Design: www.ravenstein2.de
Coverfoto: Shana Ritter
Pictures within the content: Andreas Evertz, Maresa
Mader, Shana Ritter, Dr Thomas Ritter, Sandra
Schneider
Diagramms: Alexandra Gaugl
Editor: Claudia Weingand

Printed by Graspo CZ, a.s., Czech Republic,
www.graspo.com

British Library Cataloguing in Publication Data.
A catalogue record of this book is available from the
British Library.

Printed in Czech Republic

ISBN: 978-0-85788-019-2

CONTENTS

Dr Thomas Ritter with Lipizzaner stallion Maestoso II
Shama II. (Photo: Mader)

ACKNOWLEDGEMENTS

I would like to take a brief moment to thank everyone who contributed to the realisation of this book. Above all, I would like to thank my wife, Shana Ritter, who has been supporting me tirelessly for many years. Together we developed the training method outlined in my books. In particular, the chapters on piaffe, passage and levade in this publication owe a great deal to Shana's input. Saskia and Andreas Evertz, the owners of the Aischbachhof Equestrian Centre, allowed us to use their wonderful facility for many of the photos in the book, and were helpful in many other respects as well. Their PRE stallions Amigo, Mulan and Kabul, the PRE gelding Furia, as well as their Friesian stallion Richold, are featured in many of the photos. I am also indebted to my friend and student Dr Kristen Guest, Associate Professor and Chair of English at the University of Northern British Columbia, for proofreading my English translation.

Thomas Ritter

INTRODUCTION

Lipizzaner stallion Maestoso II Catrina. (Photo: Shana Ritter)

I have studied long reining for almost three decades. I was lucky my teachers were true experts in this discipline, who passed on their knowledge as well as their passion to me. Over the years I have worked with horses of many different types and breeds on the long reins, and trained several of them to the highest levels. In the process I learned a great deal about both the individual horses and dressage training in general. My skills in the saddle also received important refinements over the decades from long reining. Gradually, long reining became one of my specialties, and I frequently presented on this topic in front of audiences. Eventually, I condensed all my experiences and observations into this book, which I have been planning for a long time and am finally able to turn into reality.

Differences between Ground Driving and Long Reining

Contrary to what some people think, long reining is traditionally considered a form of riding, not driving. That is why we talk about riding a turn or a movement on the long rein. Long reining is a type of collected work and is practised mostly at the trot and canter. For this reason, it is not really suitable for starting green horses, unlike ground driving.

Driving horses are guided by the driving reins while the driver stays a relatively large distance from the horse. In contrast to long reining, a great deal of time is spent at the walk in ground driving. The horse is tacked up with a driving harness and driving bridle, and the horse is worked on straight lines and simple turns.

In long reining, on the other hand, the horse and rider are close enough to touch. The horse wears a snaffle bridle. The reins are shorter than driving reins. The horse can learn all the movements and arena patterns of Haute Ecole, including lateral movements, flying changes, pirouettes, piaffe, and passage on the long rein.

Differences between Double Lungeing and Long Reining

Long reining also differs from double lungeing, where the horse wears a lungeing surcingle with rings through which the two lunge lines are run. In double lungeing, the trainer is usually in the centre of the circle on which the horse is moving. This circle can be moved up and down the long side of the arena. The horse is worked mostly at the trot and canter, similar to long reining.

The degree of collection, however, is typically lower than in long reining. It is very easy to make a transition from double lungeing to long reining by moving behind the horse and gradually decreasing the distance between you. This is why double lungeing is a very expedient preparation and introduction to long reining.

Lippizaner Stallion Maestoso II Shama II in trot (Photo: Shana Ritter)

WHY LONG REINING?

Advantages, Dangers, Problem Areas

Some riders will wonder why they should subject themselves to such a physically strenuous activity. For me personally, it was prompted in the beginning by my interest in being able to execute all dressage movements without sitting on the horse. As luck would have it, my teacher at the time was a real expert in this field and helped me get started.

However, there are additional reasons, besides fun and tradition, which make long reining a worthwhile pursuit. I have always found horses enjoy this type of work very much. It creates a closer bond between human and horse, as they work quite literally "side by side", and the human has to expend at least as much energy as the horse.

The rider can learn a great deal about the technical and biomechanical aspects of horse training, because they can see the horse's entire body, and especially the legs, at all times. By observing closely where each leg is and what it is doing at any given time, the rider can acquire a feel for the correct timing of the aids, which will be helpful under saddle as well. Because the rider is not sitting on the horse during long reining, they can focus on the rein aids without having to worry about the seat.

Long Reining to Support Work Under Saddle

Long reining is a great diagnostic tool, because the chain of cause and effect plays out directly before the rider's eyes. When a problem arises under saddle, you can often identify the root cause faster on the long

Fresian Stallion Richold in canter. Long reining and the work under saddle complement each other very well. (Photo: Evertz)

rein. You see the mechanics of the hind-quarters right in front of you, and it is impossible to cover up mistakes through weight and leg aids. All problems that occur under saddle will therefore show up even more clearly on the long rein. However, if the horse performs a movement better on the long reins than under saddle, it is often a sign that the rider is interfering with the horse under saddle.

The horse will improve under saddle as a direct result of long reining, and vice versa. You can explain some things better by long reining, while others can be dealt with more effectively under saddle. By the same token, the rider improves in the saddle, because they can see on the long rein what they feel in the saddle. When the

All mistakes and problems that occur under saddle tend to be seen more clearly when long reining.

rider is back in the saddle, they can match the feel in seat, legs, and reins with the visual impression obtained when long reining. In this way, both types of work benefit each other, and the rider develops a more complete and differentiated range of sensitivity.

Generally speaking, work under saddle and work on the long rein should always complement each other in a meaningful way. It is possible to teach the horse certain movements on the long reins first, without the rider's weight, before introducing them under saddle, and movements that have already been learned under saddle can be improved on the long reins so that the horse is able to perform them better when ridden. Conversely, certain aspects can be trained more effectively under saddle so the horse performs better on the long reins afterwards.

Long reining is subject to exactly the same rules and follows exactly the same principles as training under saddle. To save space I will therefore limit myself in this book to the explanation of the specific technical aspects of long reining and refer the reader to my first book, *"Classical*

The hind legs produce impulses that are transmitted forwards to the bit (blue arrows). The rider's aids send these impulses into the ground (red arrows).

Riding Based on Biomechanics" (Cadmos 2010), for matters related to riding.

Connecting the Legs with the Ground

One of the advantages of long reining is the ability to connect the horse's legs even more effectively with the ground than is possible under saddle. On one hand, the horse's back is not burdened by the rider's weight, and on the other hand, the rider is standing on the ground with their own two feet. You can find detailed information about this subject in my book "Classical Riding Based on Biomechanics". I will therefore give only a brief summary here. The trainer establishes connections between the various body parts of the horse, the aids, and the ground.

A working connection can be recognised by the free, uninhibited flow of energy impulses in all directions, from back to front, from front to back, from left to right, and from right to left. The impulses are created by the hind legs and transmitted forwards to the mouth by the musculature

The ground is the rider's most important training tool, because it anchors the aids and allows the rider to shape the horse, like a sculptor.

The hind legs create energy impulses that are transmitted forwards by the musculature and the vertebrae. The rider's aids take these impulses and send them through the horse's individual legs into the ground, which in turn bounces the horse upwards like a trampoline.

and the vertebrae (see photo on the left). The rider's aids shape and direct the horse's kinetic energy. For instance, they can push the horse into the ground like a basketball, by assigning the bulk of the body mass to a supporting leg. The ground bounces the horse upwards like a trampoline. It is indispensable for the expressiveness of the gaits, collection and fluidity that the rider is able to reach the ground with the aids through all of the horse's legs at any time. A connection cannot be established if a muscle is braced (blockage), or if it lacks tone or if it lacks positive tension (false bend). In the first case the range of motion of the affected joint is limited.

In the second case, the joint is unstable and difficult to control. In either case, the aid does not travel through the horse's body into the ground but gets stuck, so the gait cannot become elastic and springy.

Saskia Everts on the PRE Stallion Mulan in trott. As the trainer is leading the horse on the long rein, the mounted rider can feel the rein aids. (Photo: Mader)

It is, therefore, the rider's task to track down and correct any braced muscles as well as false bends in order for all theoretically-possible connections to be realised in practice.

Long Reining the Retraining Project

Just like work in hand or double lungeing, long reining can be useful in re-educating poorly trained horses. It is most suitable for forward-going horses who are very stiff. For sucked-back horses it is the wrong tool, because they will suck back even more and may even become dangerous. The trainer can also support the mounted rider very effectively from the ground with long reins in certain situations, especially if a horse does not respect half-halts or does not bend.

Further Advantages and Disadvantages of Long Reining

In lessons, the student can develop a feel for balance and a swinging back when the teacher is guiding the horse using long reins. They can feel the teacher's rein aids through their own thighs. This is also a very good method for familiarising students with dressage movements and their aids.

Horses who are returning to work after an injury that can only be worked very cautiously also benefit from long reining. Sometimes I say, only half-jokingly, that long reining is a great workout programme for the rider. Those who do it regularly burn plenty of calories and build up stamina.

> As a rule, all forms of work should complement each other in a meaningful way.

A disadvantage of long reining is that it is more difficult than under saddle to develop a good lateral bend. Also, because the dismounted rider has certain limitations in terms of speed, there is a risk that the horse begins to suck back and become stiffer. That is why horses should not be long reined exclusively. When a horse is worked under saddle regularly, the lateral bend and the desire to go forward do not get lost, and both methods can complement each other effectively.

Gelding Furia with Andreas Evertz. This was Furia's fourth time on long reins, and his first canter!

19

PREREQUISITES
for Long Reining

The Right Time

Given that the bulk of the work on long reins takes place at the collected trot and canter, it should not be started too early. Second Level dressage is a good rule of thumb. Until horses reach US Second Level they cannot collect sufficiently, which the rider has to compensate for by keeping up with the working trot and working canter. With smaller horses this is often possible within certain limits, especially if the rider is tall. However, if the horse is above a certain size, it becomes difficult. Not every rider is in good enough physical shape, or possesses the necessary leg and stride length.

The horse's ability to collect dictates how much you have to ride forward (under saddle as well as on the long rein), in order to avoid the horse sucking back and bracing. If the rider is unable to keep up with the horse's minimum speed, they will inevitably hold the horse back with the hands, which will create problems very quickly. In cases like this, one has to develop the horse's ability to collect under saddle first and postpone long reining temporarily.

The Horse

Many years ago one of my teachers was asked by an observer, after a lesson in long reining, what kind of horse was suitable for this type of work. His answer was: "An honest one". This is an extremely important point. Horses with a natural tendency to kick should obviously not be long reined. Having said that every horse has a certain natural tolerance limit, and if this limit is exceeded even the most tolerant horse will kick. Some horses' tolerance is very high, for others it is remarkably low.

The same teacher also told me that if you long rein enough, it is only a matter of time until you make a mistake and the horse kicks out. For this reason, only horses that are unshod behind should be long reined.

When something does go wrong it is best to be either out of reach behind the horse or directly next to the hind legs, so that the kick cannot develop its full force, but merely grazes the rider's thigh.

All horses kick if their tolerance limit is exceeded.

I must also warn against trying to work an unfamiliar horse on the long rein. It is important to build a relationship of mutual trust before spending time within reach of the hind legs. It is necessary for the rider to know the horse's reactions, and for the horse to be familiar with the rider's personality and way of applying the aids, so unwelcome surprises can be avoided.

The horse should be familiar with lungeing, double lungeing and work in-hand before starting with the work on long reins.

THE DRIVING AIDS

As with all advanced training methods, long reining only works with horses that are in front of the leg, or in front of the whip. Sucked-back horses are dangerous. They appear to be lazy and tired, but don't be fooled. These horses often release their pent-up energy by kicking when you try to drive them forward.

If you notice that the horse is behind the driving aids, change the strategy by bringing him honestly in front of the leg and whip again through other forms of training, in order to minimise the risk of injury, before attempting to long rein again. Lively, forward-thinking horses are therefore better suited for long reining. Horses with long, thin swan necks often tend to curl up, which is why long reining can be problematic for them. This is something that is much more difficult to cure on long reins than under saddle.

Friesian stallion Richold. Every horse can kick out. It is important to always be careful.
(Photo: Shana Ritter)

The Horse-Rider Size Ratio

The taller the rider and the shorter the horse, the easier long reining is for the rider. There are natural limits in this respect. The rider has to be able to keep up with the trotting and cantering horse while walking. The shorter the rider's legs, the more difficult this becomes. The taller the horse, the more the horse must be able to collect, so that the rider does not need to run. Running should be avoided as much as possible, because the rider has no connection with the ground during the suspension phase, which prevents the aids from coming through effectively at that moment. Traditionally, long reining horses tend to be relatively small. I prefer horses between 15hh and 16hh.

The Arena

The standard arena size of 20 m × 40 m, or 20 m × 60 m, is best suited for long reining as well as riding. The footing should be firm, yet elastic and springy. If you are forced to work in deep sand, your toes will slip back an inch or two every time you push off, which makes the work quite taxing. During the early stages a solid kick board is very important, because it is a good visual support for the inexperienced horse, and it helps the inexperienced rider to keep the horse going straight on the first track. Also, the horse cannot run very far if something goes wrong and they get loose.

The Warm-Up

The job of the warm-up phase is to establish a state of mental and physical balance for the horse, so they can focus mentally on the training. The horse is tuned carefully to the aids, just as a musical instrument is tuned before playing. The muscles are warmed-up and stretched, which is best accomplished by bending in motion.

It is important to protect the legs during the warm-up and not to waste energy, because the horse needs strength and freshness for the working phase proper, during which they are expected to learn something new and deliver an athletic performance in accordance with their level of training.

That is impossible with an exhausted horse. In addition, tired muscles can no longer support the skeleton, which means the tendons automatically take over this task. As a consequence, potentially career-ending stress injuries can ensue. At the very least, they will lead to an interruption to training for a period of several months.

Even so, many riders make the mistake of – warming their horses up – for far too long. When they are finally ready to begin the real work phase, their horses are sweaty, tired and stiff, and productive training is impossible. Chasing a stiff, unbalanced horse at the trot and canter is the fastest road to permanent lameness.

On the other hand, neither should the horse be bursting at the seams with excess energy, because they are likely to start bucking and kicking up their heels for the sheer joy of living, thereby posing a life-threatening hazard for the person at the end of the long reins.

Long reining itself can be used to warm-up the horse before riding. However, if long reining is intended to occupy the main working phase, it does not hurt to lunge the horse first for a few minutes. Work in-hand is also a good preparation for the horse. The Portuguese variety is especially suitable, because you can make a seamless transition from work in-hand to long reining this way (see the chapter on "Portuguese-Style Work In-Hand"). The warm-up method chosen depends on the horse's temperament, their training level and how they feel on that particular day.

STRETCHING

Before beginning work in-hand it can be a good idea to stretch the horse's neck

The purpose of the warm-up is to prepare the horse for the work and to tune them to the aids. It must never devolve into mechanically wearing the horse out.

muscles with flexion exercises (see photos) in order to find and, if necessary, remove blockages in the throatlatch area and poll, because stiff neck and poll muscles block the back and the hind legs. Without this preparation, horses easily get behind the driving aids and do not come on the bit. It is therefore useful to return to these exercises periodically during the later training stages in order to restore or improve the

Lungeing helps to balance the horse mentally and physically in order to prepare them for the workout proper. This is the Friesian stallion Richold on the lunge line wearing a snaffle, cavesson, side reins and lungeing surcingle, as is the tradition in the Spanish Riding School of Vienna. (Photo: Shana Ritter)

Flexion, i.e. mobilisation of the upper cervical vertebrae by stretching the outside neck muscles, demonstrated by the PRE stallion Toledano. (Photos: Evertz)

mobility of the poll. In Prussian and Austrian cavalry regiments, it was customary to spend several minutes every day on dismounted flexion exercises before training under saddle, and the training sessions themselves were frequently interrupted by mounted as well as dismounted flexion exercises.

The Horse's Equipment

THE SNAFFLE

The traditional long-reining bridle is the full-cheek snaffle with a dropped noseband. You can use a loose-ring or eggbutt snaffle as an alternative. The bit can be single or double jointed. Curb bits are not used, because the design of the curb bit makes it difficult to encourage the horse to bend, and can suppress the horse's desire to go forward.

THE CAVESSON

The long reins are usually attached to the snaffle bit, but there are situations in which it is convenient to attach the long reins to the rings of a cavesson. I use this variation especially when supporting a rider from the ground. This arrangement has the advantage that the rider establishes a connection with the horse through the bit, while I can address the nose. In horses with a difficult poll conformation it can sometimes be helpful to attach the long reins to the cavesson instead of the snaffle.

The cavesson should be designed as follows. The nose piece consists of a single piece of metal to which three moveable rings are attached. This nose piece should not be padded too thickly, because fine aids would be absorbed and only crude aids penetrate the heavy padding. Portuguese cavessons and the cavesson of the Spanish Riding School are the most suitable.

THE LONG REINS

To cut to the chase: there are currently no suitable long reins available in tack shops. They are usually much too long and are reminiscent of a double lunge line. Some riders convert draw reins into long reins, but this is rarely a good solution because draw reins are too short for most horses. You either have to sew your own long reins or have them made by a harness maker. You should choose a material that is soft enough to allow you to feel the horse well. It should not be too smooth, so that the reins cannot slip through the trainer's fingers when wearing gloves.

I personally like to work with cotton, because it does not readily cause rope burns if the horse should leap forward suddenly, and because it allows a good feel for the horse's body. Harsh materials are not suitable.

The width of the reins should fit the size of the rider's hands, which means that riders with large hands will probably prefer wider reins, whereas smaller riders with petite hands need a narrower rein. If the

The correctly-adjusted cavesson offers the possibility of attaching either the long reins or the lead rein of the assistant, when supporting the horse's first steps on the long reins. (Photo: Mader)

width of the reins does not fit the width of the fingers it will become uncomfortable, which in turn interferes with the rider's concentration on the horse. For effective work, it is important the reins feel comfortable in the rider's hand.

The long reins end either in a piece of leather with a metal buckle, or in a metal clip that is attached to the snaffle ring. As far as the colour is concerned, I mainly use black in training. For exhibitions you can choose a colour that matches the pad, if you are using one. You can also match the colour of the reins to the colour of the horse, so that it becomes as invisible as possible. This creates the illusion that the horse is performing by himself, while the rider merely happens to be walking next to him.

REIN LENGTH

The long reins should not be too long. There are many so-called "long reins" that are more like double lunge lines. They are so long you have to hold many unwieldy loops in your hands when you are close to the horse's haunches. In addition, long reins often end in thin, round ropes that can extend all the way from the bit to the haunches. This part is too thin to permit a good feel in the rider's hand, and this is why these reins are suitable for double lungeing but not for long reining. The optimal length of the reins depends a little on the horse's height and training level. If the rein is too short, it limits the rider's mobility too much. If it is too long, it becomes unwieldy. I prefer a length that surrounds the horse comfortably with one loop in my hand, when I am directly beside the croup. Such a rein has a length of approximately 15–18 ft (5–6 m).

USE A LUNGE LINE IN THE BEGINNING

When I start a new horse and want to maintain a greater distance, I use a lunge

It is important for the success of the work that the rein feels comfortable in the rider's hand. (Photo: Thomas Ritter)

line as a long rein. Only lunge lines with a loop on one end are suitable for this, because you need to be able to thread the end with the clip through the loop. Push the loop through one of the snaffle rings, then thread the clip through the loop and pull the entire lunge line through it, until it tightens around the snaffle ring. The clip is then attached to the other snaffle ring. Don't forget to untwist the lunge line! Lunge lines without a swivel joint are most suitable, because they cannot twist by themselves. The swivel joint also makes this end a little heavier, which changes the feel to some extent.

LUNGEING SURCINGLE AND PAD

Using a lungeing surcingle only makes sense if you want to maintain a considerable distance from the horse for safety reasons. When you are walking behind the horse at a distance, the long reins can be run through the rings on the sides of the surcingle to prevent the reins from dropping too low or sliding across the back, if the horse tries to turn around. This improves the stability of the rein contact. However, as soon as the training has reached the stage where you can walk next to the croup or directly behind it, flexibility is paramount. You need to be able to carry the reins higher or lower, or to run them across the horse's back. Rings and tackle rolls limit this flexibility and make the job harder rather than easier.

Pads are used mainly for exhibitions, not for training. They serve no practical purpose and are purely decorative in nature. They are smaller than regular saddle pads and should not have keepers for the saddle etc. Only a girth is required to keep the pad in place.

SIDE REINS

Some trainers use side reins in the beginning of the training with inexperienced riders and with horses who don't come on the bit easily. My own experiences with them have not been very positive, for two reasons.

On the one hand, side reins hinder the horse's desire to go forward, which is especially serious on long reins, because horses tend to suck back more easily on long reins than under saddle. On the other hand, they do not allow enough lateral bend and limit the lateral flexibility of the neck, thereby preventing the rider from suppling the horse by encouraging them to bend in motion or at the halt.

Thus, side reins make the work more difficult. Problems with poll flexion can be resolved more effectively through correct gymnastic work.

The Rider's Equipment

BOOTS AND GLOVES

Given that long reining is weightless riding, the same dress code tradition applies as in riding: either tall boots and breeches, or jodhpurs and short boots. I have to admit, however, that tall leather boots are not made for walking and suffer very much from long reining, especially if you are walking in sand footing. It is therefore understandable if you want to protect your good riding boots by wearing something else. From a safety standpoint, there are a few general rules to consider; for instance, you should wear firm shoes that cover the ankles. Otherwise, you can easily rub your ankles and create open sores, or the horse's hind hoof may accidentally brush against you, which can cause injury. A solid boot offers better protection against twisted ankles as well. Steel-reinforced toes are not a bad idea, because the rider's foot can end up underneath the horse's hind hoof when working at close quarters. Open sandals and running shoes are completely unsuitable for these reasons. Solid, tall hiking boots, military style boots or construction boots fulfil the safety requirements.

The use of gloves is a matter of personal preference. A horse that drags the rider along is not really ready for long reining yet. I myself wear gloves only in cold weather. When it is very warm, I find them uncomfortable. I prefer leather gloves that are sturdy and allow a good feel.

THE WHIP

The length of the whip depends on the rider's position. The greater the distance from the horse, the longer the whip should be. If you are far enough away to be out of reach of the hind legs, for instance, you may have to use a lunge whip in order to be able to reach the horse with the lash of the whip. If you close the distance to approximately 6–7 ft (about 2 m), a driving whip will be sufficient. Once you have arrived at the hindquarters, you can exchange the driving whip for a dressage whip. Sometimes it is advantageous to use a relatively short riding crop, in order to be able to switch it easily from one hand to the other, without getting it caught on the horse.

PRE stallion Kabul with Shana Ritter. A straight posture with engaged core muscles is necessary when long reining as well as when riding. (Photo: Thomas Ritter)

THE RIDER'S
Posture and Position

Always Stay Balanced

It is important for the rider to be balanced at all times. The torso should therefore be kept vertically above the pelvis, as this is the only position that allows independent use of the arms and legs. As soon as the rider loses their balance, for instance by tipping too far forward, they can neither support the horse nor give clear instructions. The connection between the hands, the core muscles and the weight, as well as the grounding of the rider's weight, is then lost. It is the core muscles that mainly control the balance. If the rider tips forward, perhaps because they are out of breath, they should stop and rest, and continue only after taking a short break. It is better to do short reprises of high quality work than long reprises of poor quality work.

THE USE OF THE "SEAT"

Seat aids are just as important in lungeing, work in-hand and long reining as in riding. This may sound paradoxical at first, because you are not sitting on the horse. But the aids can only be transmitted when they originate in the core muscles, and when they are anchored by the core muscles.

This is the case only if the elbows are connected to the hips, and the rider's core muscles are engaged. Otherwise the aids lack the necessary cohesiveness, get stuck somewhere in the horse's body, and do not make sense to the horse. As in riding, the elbows should not move too far from the body, because this weakens the connection between the core and the hand, which puts too much strain on the rider's shoulders, stiffens the wrists, and encourages the horse to fight the rein aids.

For a better understanding it helps to get insight from Asian cultures. The core ("Kreuz" in German) is closely related to the term "hara", which is used in martial arts. It represents engagement of the abdominal and back muscles, which lowers the centre of gravity and improves the person's balance considerably. The stability gained in this way allows the person to keep their arm and leg muscles loose and relaxed. Weak core muscles, on the other hand, lead to poor balance. The prin-

Lipizzaner stallion Maestoso II Shama II in the canter. The effect of the seat allows the rider to create an elastic, positive, resilient tension along the horse's spine and to channel his energy upwards into an uphill canter. (Photo: Mader)

Even while long reining the rider needs to use his seat in order for the aids to be effective.

ciple I have just outlined briefly applies to lungeing, work in-hand and long reining, as much as to the mounted rider.

THE CONNECTION TO THE GROUND

The rider uses the support of the ground to help ensure that the half-halts are transmitted. The way in which this works is to push one heel firmly into the ground during the half-halt. This creates a connection from the bit through the rein, and the rider's body to the ground, which makes the rein aid more effective. Should the horse push against the half-halting hand with the croup or neck, they will encounter the resistance of the ground. The rider's hand is then merely a link in a chain, and the horse half-halts on their own. Using this method, you can stop even large, strong horses if something goes wrong and the horse tries to bolt. If the rider loses their connection with the ground, however, even a small horse can unbalance them and drag them along.

In effect, the rider is able to feel the energy of the pushing hindquarters in the reins and channel it into the ground like a lightning rod. With the help of this grounding, pushing power can be transformed into carrying power.

The Rider's Position

There are different traditions regarding the rider's position with respect to the horse. At the Spanish Riding School in Vienna it is customary for the rider to walk next to the inside hind leg, or slightly behind it, in the walk and trot on a single track and when performing the shoulder-in. In the canter, haunches-in, renvers, and half pass the rider walks next to the outside hind leg, and in the piaffe and passage they stay in the middle, directly behind the horse.

At Egon von Neindorff's Riding Institute it was customary to stay more in the middle, behind the horse, and deviate only very slightly to either side.

ADVANTAGES AND DISADVANTAGES OF THE DIFFERENT POSITIONS

I personally seek the position in which I can influence the individual horse most effectively.

Next page:
PRE stallion Amigo with Andreas Evertz. In the Spanish Riding School tradition the rider walks on the inside in single track work and in the shoulder-in.
(Photo: Shana Ritter)

Stallion Amigo with Andreas Evertz. At Egon von Neindorff's Institute it was customary to stay centred behind the horse.

PRE Stallion Amigo with Andreas Evertz. If the rider walks next to the outside hind leg, they can ask the inside hind leg to engage by bringing it closer with the inside rein. (Photos: Shana Ritter)

Walking in the middle, behind the horse, you can frame them on both sides with the reins. You are also able to apply the driving aids more easily in this position. When you are working without the support of an arena kickboard, it is easier to keep the horse straight when you are directly behind them. With horses from whom you want to maintain a greater distance, it makes sense to stay in the middle for the same reason. As the distance from the horse increases, the precision of the aids decreases if you are off to the side.

When walking close behind the horse, the rider will occasionally step on the horse's heels by accident, because the horse is not sufficiently engaged and the hind legs do not stay far enough underneath the body. As soon as the hind legs engage more and flex under the body mass, the problem disappears.

If the horse tends to fall in from the outside school track or circle towards the inside, they can be kept on the line of travel more effectively if the rider walks next to the outside hind leg.

The inside rein, run low, frames the inside hind leg and rib cage and pushes the horse towards the outside. The general rule of thumb in situations like this is that it is easier to "lift" the horse closer to oneself than to push them away. For example, on his stiffer side, the inexperienced horse

often drifts away from the kickboard to the inside of the arena, falling on to the inside shoulder. They will return to the track much more easily if you walk on the outside, between the wall and the horse, than if you are on the inside trying to push them out.

In the next training step it is possible to walk in the middle, behind the horse. The inside rein runs between the inside stifle and the point of the inside hip, framing the inside shoulder. The outside rein runs across the middle of the croup.

If the croup tends to deviate from the line of travel, this can often be prevented very effectively by walking next to the hind leg on the hollow side to block it from escaping laterally. If the croup drifts towards the inside, it is better to walk on the inside. If the croup drifts towards the outside, on the other hand, it is better to walk between the wall and the outside hind leg. The rider can thus control the hip that moves toward them and the diagonal shoulder that wants to move away from them.

During training, you should walk in the position from which you can influence the horse most effectively under the circumstances.

THE AIDS

Differences between Long Reining and Work Under Saddle

While the aids are in principle the same for all forms of horse training, long reining only allows for the use of rein, voice and whip aids. In addition, it makes sense to use the back of the hand, the forearm, the shoulder, or even the hip in certain moments to communicate with the horse. The system of used aids in long reining Lipizzaner is thus more flexible than those used under saddle.

Certain things never change, however. The driving aids, for instance, bring the horse to the reins on long reins as well as under saddle. These receive the energy and return it to the hindquarters – developing an energy circuit. The inside aids support the bend, while the outside aids support the turn.

The only available driving aids for use with long reins are the whip and the voice. Besides these, the trainer's posture and concentration play a vital role. If you grow tall and engage your core muscles, the horse will respond by growing taller in front and making contact with the reins. If the rider is too limp, the horse will be deflated before too long as well.

Lipizzaner stallion Conversano Sorria with Shana Ritter in the trot half-pass. (Photo: Thomas Ritter)

Voice Commands

The voice can have a driving or a soothing effect. A short, energetic aid with a rising intonation contour has a more driving effect. A longer, sustained, deeper voice aid with a falling intonation contour has a more soothing effect.

You can teach the horse certain voice commands before beginning work on long reins. These can then serve as a mental bridge to understanding the physical aids. As with work on the lunge you could, for instance, explain the transitions between the gaits to the horse by combining familiar voice commands with the regular aids at first. Once the horse understands the physical aids, the voice commands can be dropped.

Whip Aids

The whip can be used in a variety of ways. It can have an invigorating, forward-driving effect, but it can also drive sideways, support turns and frame the horse. The desired effect of the aid, as well as the rider's position, determines how to hold the whip.

VERTICAL WHIP, TIP POINTING DOWN

When walking next to the horse, it is usually most convenient to hold the whip as you would in the saddle, with the tip pointing down, because you can reach the horse most easily this way and touch the lateral hind leg on the outside, from behind or, if you are very skilled, from the inside.

VERTICAL WHIP, TIP POINTING UP

The centred position, directly behind the horse (perhaps with a slightly greater distance), lends itself well to carrying the whip vertically, with the tip pointing up. When holding the whip in this way, you touch the horse either on top of the croup or on the side of the hip. If you are close enough to touch the horse with your hands it is more effective to have the tip of the whip pointing down.

HORIZONTAL WHIP

The horizontal whip can touch the horse's rib cage, where the rider's calf normally rests. This is recommended for horses who might kick. The horse responds to the touch of the whip on the rib cage by lengthening their strides or by turning the shoulders, whereas touching the side of the hind leg with the vertical whip (tip pointing down)

Aids must be applied as impulses. They have to breathe with the horse. Without repeated timely releases, everything inevitably gets stuck in a gridlock.

Friesian stallion Richold demonstrating work in-hand. The rider's inside hand holds the inside rein just behind the snaffle ring. The outside hand holds the outside rein and the whip. (Photo: Mader)

tends to result in sidestepping or lifting the hind leg higher.

The rider should experiment to find out where to touch the horse with the whip for the best results, because they will be different for each situation. You will have to touch the horse in a different place for a circle than for a shoulder-in or a half pass, since both the demands made on the animal and the contents of the communication are different. There is a great deal of creative freedom in this area as well.

THE ACTIVATING WHIP AID

The invigorating, activating whip aid consists of a vibration. Let the horse feel the weight of the whip first to draw their attention to the coming driving aid. Then vibrate with the whip against the horse's coat – it is the speed of the vibration that makes the aid effective. The final touch can be a little stronger than the preceding ones. (For the tuning of the horse to the whip aid, see *"Classical Riding Based on Biomechanics"*).

Lipizzaner stallion Maestoso II Shama II. The horizontally placed whip can frame the horse, drive him, or turn the shoulder. (Photo: Mader)

This activating aid can be applied either in the position of the rider's leg on the rib cage, on top of the croup, on the side of the hind leg, or even on the inside of the hind leg.

THE FRAMING WHIP AID

Just as the rider's leg can have a framing effect on the horse under saddle, the whip can have a framing effect in long reining. For this purpose, it is best to hold it hori-

zontally and press it against the rib cage or the side of the horse's hip to prevent any lateral evasion. You can simultaneously squeeze the rein lightly against the rib cage or the side of the hip.

THE LATERALLY DRIVING WHIP

The whip drives sideways when it is applied on the side of the hip or on the outside of a hind leg. I always combine this whip aid with pressure applied using the rein, a finger, or the back of my hand against the side of the horse's pelvis. I like to tune my horses to yield to a slight lateral pressure of the rein against their pelvis.

THE TURNING WHIP AID

Turns can be supported by squeezing the horizontal whip together with the outside rein against the outside of the rib cage. The whip has a turning effect in this situation. Sometimes it helps to activate the inside hind leg and engage it under the centre of gravity in turns. The horse then accepts the turning outside rein better.

Rein Aids

The long reins have all the same functions as the rein aids under saddle, but in addition they take on certain jobs that normally fall to the rider's leg aids. They are used not only for bending, turning, and half-halting, but also to frame a shoulder or a hind leg, to drive laterally, and even to drive forward in certain situations.

Lipizzaner stallion Conversano Sorria in a turn that is supported by the horizontally-placed whip in the outside hand. (Photo: Mader)

I have to address the safety aspect again here. Every horse kicks. Some kick sooner, and some kick later. Some horses are extremely patient and only kick out when the rider is excessively aggressive. Others are much more irritable and may kick out against a very subtle driving aid.

Excessive energy can also become dangerous, for instance, if a horse starts bucking. This desire to move should be fulfilled in the pasture, in a controlled fashion on the lunge line, or under saddle before starting to long rein.

It is also crucial to develop your feel for the horse as much as possible, in order to judge accurately how much you may ask of your horse and with what intensity you can, may or must apply the aids.

HOLDING THE REINS

Traditionally, the long reins are held the same way as the reins under saddle, i.e. coming from the horse's mouth they run between the ring finger and little finger, up through the palm, and exit towards the front between the thumb and index finger. Alternatively, it is often comfortable to run them in from the front, either between thumb and index finger or between index and middle finger, into the palm and down. I personally find that this allows a very good feel for the horse's body. It also makes the reins run in a straighter line in many cases so that the aids are directed horizontally rather than slanted downwards.

Most long reins are so long that you have to hold the loops of surplus rein in one hand. I hold the loops of rein in one hand and the whip in the other. Otherwise, it gets too unwieldy.

The reins can be held in a variety of positions and heights. There are some simple rules of thumb.

PRE stallion Amigo with Andreas Evertz in a leg yield on the diagonal at the trot. The low-running rein is able to frame the lateral hind leg or drive it sideways.
(Photo: Shana Ritter)

Lipizzaner stallion Conversano Sorria with Shana Ritter in counter shoulder-in. The high outside rein makes room for the haunches to sidestep.
(Photo: Mader)

- The lower the rein runs along the hind leg, the more efficiently it can frame the leg laterally and, if necessary, drive it sideways.

- The higher the rein runs, the more it allows for the lateral hind leg to step sideways. In some lateral movements, a high rein makes it easier for the horse to understand the rider's intentions. Applied at the wrong time, however, a high rein allows the horse to evade the rider's aids by getting crooked and escaping laterally with the hind legs.

Lipizzaner stallion Conversano Sorria with Thomas Ritter in counter shoulder-in. The high outside rein makes room for the haunches to sidestep.
(Photo: Mader)

- Running one rein diagonally across the back brings the horse's shoulder closer to the rider and enables the rider to push the croup away.

Lipizzaner stallion Maestoso II Shama II in a haunches-in canter. The inside rein running diagonally across the back can frame the inside shoulder, position the horse to the inside, and simultaneously make the croup yield to the inside.
(Photo: Mader)

- Pressing downwards on top of the croup with the rein can flex the joints of the grounded hind leg in both the half- and the full halt.

Lipizzaner stallion Maestoso II Shama II. Pressing down onto the croup with the rein can make the horse lower his croup.
(Photo: Mader)

- Both reins running snugly along either side of the rib cage and pelvis can frame the hindquarters and keep them on the track, like two guard rails.

FRAMING REIN AIDS

In order to straighten the horse and guide them on precise lines, the rider needs to be able to frame the horse. This is much easier under saddle than on long reins, because the mounted rider has reins, knees, thighs, and calves available for this purpose.

FRAMING THE SHOULDERS AND RIB CAGE

You can frame the left shoulder on long reins by walking next to the right hind leg and running the left rein across the back. In this way, it is possible to guide the left shoulder towards the right with tactful aids of the left rein, without bending the horse to the left. Simultaneously, you can prevent the right hind leg from escaping to the right from your position beside the horse. This is important, because you can move the shoulder laterally only if you can keep the hind legs on their line of travel, and vice versa.

Walking behind the horse, you can run the left rein across the back to the inside and "hook" it around the point of the inside hip, in order to frame the left shoulder. The inside hip is thus connected to the outside shoulder, and they can be aligned with each other. The inside rein can then create lateral poll flexion, if needed.

The left side of the rib cage can be framed by creating a close contact with the left rein running horizontally along the horse's barrel, and pulsating it against the rib cage when it is swinging to the right. Touching the horse with the horizontally-placed whip where the mounted rider's leg would be can support the rein aid if needed. In addition, the whip can produce pressure or a vibration. The rider should walk either behind the horse or next to the right hind leg for this exercise. The more the left hind leg engages, the less the rib cage will drift to the left

FRAMING A HIND LEG

There are several different ways to frame a hind leg. Let us assume again that the horse is hollow right, so their shoulders drift to the left and the haunches drift to the right as a result of their natural crookedness. The right hind leg is framed and prevented from escaping laterally by the rider walking next to it, running the left rein across the middle of the back and pushing the right hind leg a little to the left with the back of the left hand and the left forearm, as if wanting to ask for a haunches-in (or half-pass, or renvers, respectively, depending on whether the inside or outside hind leg is involved). Sometimes it is enough merely to walk next to the hind leg of the hollow side.

If the inside hind leg escapes in a half-pass, however, it is more effective to walk behind the horse and drive the inside hind leg straight forward. The inside rein then runs across the middle of the croup, rather than across the middle of the back, to the outside. If necessary it can be placed against the horse's inside hip in order to prevent the angle from becoming too steep.

If the hindquarters drift to the inside on a circle, the rider can walk on the inside and bring the outside shoulder a little to the inside with the outside rein, while pushing the inside hind leg towards the outside with the whip and the outside hand (which is next to the horse's inside hip).

> *The lower the rein runs along the side of the horse, the more effectively the hind leg of that side can be framed or engaged if needed.*

Lipizzaner stallion Conversano Sorria at the end of a trot half-pass. The left rein is framing the left shoulder and is asking the right hind leg to engage. (Photo: Mader)

One must note, however, that in this position the horse may evade the attempt at straightening by making the circle smaller. In this case, it is better to walk next to the outside hind leg and carry the inside rein low, i.e. just above the hock. In this way the inside hind leg can be "leveraged" towards the outside. This approach is generally more successful than trying to push the horse away to the outside, because the whip in the inside hand helps frame the horse.

BENDING REIN AIDS

A bending rein aid addresses mainly the horse's spine. It is aimed at stretching the muscles on the outside of the bend. Just as with riding, the bending rein aid can be applied either when the front leg or the hind leg on the same side is on the ground. The horse's reactions will often be different, depending on the phase of the footfall sequence during which the aid is applied.

Some horses let the rein aid go through- better with their front legs, others with their hind legs.

BENDING THE CERVICAL SPINE

By letting the bending rein aid go through, the horse yields with no resistance. The cervical spine bends precisely where and to the degree indicated by the rider's aids. To be effective, however, the bending rein aid must travel through the leg that is being addressed and into the ground. This means the shoulder muscles have to cooperate. If a hind leg is targeted, the abdominal muscles and hip muscles on the same side of the body must be relaxed for the aid to go through the horse's body without getting stuck. One indication of the aid being trans- mitted is that the rider will be able to stop the horse into this particular leg without any resistance; another is that the gait becomes more elastic after the bending aid if the horse is in motion.

Lipizzaner stallion Conversano Sorria in a turn. The longer the outside rein is kept, the more the horse bends the base of his neck. The shorter the outside rein is kept, the more the lateral bend is limited to the throatlatch area. (Photo: Mader)

Some horses let the aids go through better with their outside legs, others with their inside legs. Often there is a diagonal correlation: one diagonal pair of legs lets the aids go through better than the other one. The goal of the training is to make all legs equally permeable to the aids (see the section on half-halts and full halts).

The basic rules for bending are the same as in riding. One rein asks the horse to yield laterally by bending the neck or poll, while the opposite rein frames and limits the bend at the same time, to prevent the horse from overbending or bending in the wrong part of the neck.

CORRECT RIB CAGE BEND

One of the great challenges of long reining lies in achieving a correct rib cage bend. This is done on circles and in corners at the beginning, while walking behind or next to

The longer the outside rein is kept, the more the base of the neck is included in the bend. The shorter the outside rein is kept, the more the bend is limited to the poll and the upper third of the neck.

the outside hind leg. The inside rein and the horizontally held whip touch the inside of the rib cage. The whip can drive the inside hind leg forwards if necessary, and together with the inside rein it pushes the horse into the outside rein. These driving aids alternate with bending aids that are applied when one of the inside legs has touched down, as mentioned above.

The practical and technical details of the bending rein aids vary slightly, depending on the exact position of the rider. When walking directly behind the horse, I like to run both reins along the top or the sides of the croup, as this allows me to frame the horse more effectively with the outside rein, and to prevent the base of the neck from overbending. The inside (bending) rein is then able to determine very precisely where the horse will bend.

With the rider walking next to the inside hind leg, the outside rein runs across the middle of the back, framing the base of the neck, while the rider's outside forearm together with the back of the outside hand prevent the inside hind leg from escaping to the inside. The inside rein can then be used in an opening fashion to stretch the outside of the neck.

Walking next to the outside hind leg, you can keep the outside rein close to the horse to prevent the haunches from drifting out. In the haunches-in and half-pass I often move the outside rein slightly away from the horse towards the outside, in order to push the croup towards the inside with my inside hand. The inside rein is then

Lipizzaner stallion Maestoso II Shama II. Both reins run along the side of the horse's hips, allowing the rider to determine the lateral poll flexion very precisely. (Photos: Shana Ritter)

Lipizzaner stallion Maestoso II Shama II. Here, the outside rein is run across the middle of the back towards the inside, in order to frame the outside shoulder and the inside hind leg at the same time, so the horse cannot become crooked.

run across the middle of the back, and the rider's inside forearm and the back of the inside hand can touch the horse's outside hind leg in order to steady the hand during bending aids. The inside rein then has a framing effect on the inside shoulder as well as a bending effect.

HALF-HALTS

The purpose of a half-halt is to keep a certain leg on the ground for a split second longer than usual. If it is a hind leg, its joints are supposed to flex, as a person would when doing a squat. A series of three half-halts is used to produce a transition into a lower gait or to the halt.

Just as with the bending rein aids, half-halts can address an individual leg. It is also possible to connect a specific leg with the ground – i.e. keep it on the ground for a split second longer. I often compare this to a 'fermata', or a dotted note in music, in which the note is sustained for slightly longer.

It is crucially important to distinguish between half-halts and bending rein aids. For instance, it is possible to half-halt on the outside rein without bending the horse to the outside.

The difference between a bending rein aid and a half-halt is the rider's intention on the one hand, and their technique on the other. For a bending aid, the rein is shortened slightly. The hand can also leave its place, if necessary. The opposite rein will have to release a little. In a half-halt,

A bending or positioning rein aid addresses the horse's spine. A half halt, on the other hand, addresses a specific leg. Bending and half-halting rein aids are therefore not identical. For instance, you can half-halt with the right rein while positioning the horse to the left.

the hand remains in place. Its fingers are temporarily closed more firmly, and the opposite rein gives a bit more support.

As a general rule, the more the rein can rest against the horse's body, the greater is its framing effect, and the more precisely it transmits the aids. For this reason, I like to rest my hand on the croup during a half-halt, when walking behind the horse. When I am too far away from the horse for this, I often let the half-halting rein rest on top of the croup – which also lends my hand more stability.

When walking on the inside, I press my outside hand slightly against the horse's inside hip during a half-halt if the horse

Next page: Lipizzaner stallion Maestoso II Shama II. The rider must differentiate carefully between half-halts and bending rein aids. (Photo: Shana Ritter)

shows a tendency to drift towards the inside with the hindquarters.

LATERALLY DRIVING REIN AIDS

This is an area in which long reining differs from riding. For many riders it will probably come as a surprise to learn that the rein can be used as a driving aid. This is a peculiarity of long reining. There are several different ways to apply lateral driving aids.

ENLARGING THE CIRCLE

On curved arena patterns the rider can walk on the outside next to the croup, while running the inside rein between the inside hock and stifle and around the inside hind leg. While it is swinging forwards, the trajectory of the inside hind leg can be redirected towards the outside shoulder by bringing it closer to the rider's body with the inside rein. This feels as though you are lifting the horse towards yourself. The

Lipizzaner stallion Conversano Sorria. The inside rein is run across the horse's back towards the outside. It bends the horse in turns and prevents him from falling onto his inside shoulder. The outside rein turns the shoulder and prevents the outside hind leg from drifting out. (Photo: Mader)

whip can be used simultaneously as a supporting, enhancing aid.

TURNING

Walking behind the horse, the outside, turning rein can be lowered to just above the outside hock. In this way, it can squeeze laterally against the outside hind leg to guide it towards the inside. The aid is always applied when the hind leg is in the air. This is the only time at which the path of the leg can be influenced. The outside rein can support the turn initially by guiding the outside hind leg forwards and inwards. This is an aid that is generally only necessary in the early stages of training. Later, the horse can be turned by an invisible taking and yielding of the outside rein in its normal position.

LATERAL MOVEMENTS

From behind the horse it is possible to push the inside hind leg forwards and outwards with pressure of the lowered inside rein. The aid can be enhanced by walking on the outside.

When the rider is walking behind the horse in a half-pass, the outside rein can apply lateral pressure against the outside hind leg, around the top of the stifle joint, in order to engage it.

When the rider is walking on the outside, the inside rein is run across the middle of the back and is able to push the outside hind leg sideways if necessary.

ALL THESE LATERAL DRIVING AIDS CAN BE SUPPORTED BY THE WHIP.

In the haunches-in and renvers, the rider usually walks next to the outside hind leg. The lateral driving aid is the same as in the half-pass.

FORWARD DRIVING REIN AIDS

The forward driving rein aid is used more rarely in practice than the vibration of the

Lipizzaner stallion Conversano Sorria with Shana Ritter in shoulder-in. The rider is walking on the inside. (Photo: Mader)

Lipizzaner stallion Maestoso II Shama II in a trot half-pass. The rider is walking in the centre behind the horse.

Lipizzaner stallion Maestoso II Shama II in a trot half-pass. The rider is walking next to the outside hind leg. (Photos: Mader)

whip, because it is only applicable in certain situations. It works best when walking next to the outside hind leg on a circle, with the inside rein running low around the inside hind leg. The moment the inside hind leg leaves the ground, the rider can apply pressure with the inside rein from back to front, thereby pushing the hind leg forward. Because the hand is moving forward, it yields the horse's mouth to the appropriate degree, so there is no contradiction between the driving aid and the rein contact. Some riders slap one rein against the hind leg as a warning if the horse is not moving forward with enough energy. Although this can work, it is crucial not to yank on the horse's mouth at the same time by accident, since they would not understand the instruction. Driving while simultaneously punishing the horse for going forward is unfair and counterproductive. Because few riders are coordinated enough to apply this slapping rein aid without interfering with the horse's mouth, I would advise against it. The driving voice and whip aids are safer.

Summary

I want to summarize the most important points about the aids and the rider's position here.

As you can see in the tables, there are essentially three different positions for the whip, the rider, and the reins. All of these positions have advantages and disadvantages. You therefore have to find the most suitable position for yourself, the reins, and the whip for each situation, in order to apply the aids with the highest possible efficacy. If you cannot communicate your point effectively in one position, you must keep looking for another until you find the right one.

WHIP POSITION

There are basically three different variations:
• Vertical with the tip pointing up
• Vertical with the tip pointing down
• Horizontal along the rib cage

The vertical position with the tip pointing up is generally used when walking behind the horse at a distance of approximately the length of the dressage whip. You can use it to touch the top of the croup to make the gait livelier.

In the half-pass, the rider can walk on the outside of the horse and reach across the top of the croup to touch the inside hind leg.

The vertical position with the tip pointing down is most practical when the rider is walking right next to the horse, and wants to touch a hind leg. If you touch the back of the hind leg, the aid has a forward driving effect. If you touch the outside of the hind leg, the whip can drive the horse sideways. This movement requires the coordination of the reins and the rider's entire body language.

The whip held horizontally against the rib cage is most suitable when the rider is walking more or less behind the horse. It

Lipizzaner stallion Conversano Sorria with Shana Ritter in the counter-canter. The whip has a framing function here. (Photo: Mader)

Whip Position	Situation
Tip pointing up	• Rider behind the horse • Rider not close enough to touch the horse • Forward driving aid
Tip pointing down	• Rider close enough to touch the horse • Forward driving aid • Lateral driving aid
Horizontal along the rib cage	• Rider behind rather than next to the horse • Framing aid • Turning aid • Lateral driving aid

has a forwards-sideways driving effect in the shoulder-in, in the corner, and in enlarging the circle.

On the outside it helps turn the outside shoulder and has a framing effect. For the rider's position there are also three basic possibilities:

• Next to the outside hind leg
• In the centre behind the horse
• Next to the inside hind leg

The position next to the outside hind leg enables the rider to use their body to prevent the hind leg from escaping. In addition, the outside shoulder can be turned with the outside rein that is run horizontally, and with the support of the whip. This position also allows the engagement of the inside hind leg to enlarge the circle or for a shoulder-in, with the inside rein that is run on the inside of the horse's body. Bending

RIDER POSITION

Rider Position	Application
On the outside, next to the horse	• Bending • Enlarging the circle • Engaging the inside hind leg • Framing the inside shoulder • Framing the outside hind leg with one's body • Haunches-in/Half-pass • Canter in Viennese tradition
In the centre behind the horse	• Straightening • Driving forward • Piaffe • Passage • Levade • Tempo changes
On the inside next to the horse	• Framing the outside shoulder • Framing the inside hind leg through one's own body • Framing the outside hind leg with the outside rein

of the rib cage can also be developed more effectively in this way. From the position next to the outside hind leg it is especially easy to move the croup to the inside and to engage the outside hind leg in the haunches-in, in the renvers, and in the half pass. For this purpose, the inside rein is run across the middle of the horse's back to the outside. In the Spanish Riding School the horse is led from the outside in the canter.

The centred rider position behind the horse is especially suitable for two-legged and four-legged beginners. It enables the rider to be effective in framing the horse laterally on both sides, and to send the horse forward on a straight line of travel. Should it be necessary to lengthen the stride, this position is the most useful. For piaffe, passage, levade and tempi changes at the canter, this position is also generally the most effective.

PRE stallion Kabul with Shana Ritter. Walking next to the inside hind leg is the standard position in the Spanish Riding School for the walk and the trot on a single track. (Photo: Thomas Ritter)

Austrian warmblood mare Bayenne with Evi Petrak. (Photo: Schneider)

REIN POSITION

Rein Position	Application
Running along the side of the horse's pelvis	• Framing the hindquarters • Turning • Driving laterally
Running along the top of the pelvis	• Lowering the croup • Yielding to "open the door" for the lateral hind leg • Framing a shoulder • Framing a hind leg by pressure of the hand next to the dock of the tail
Running diagonally across the back	• Framing the diagonal shoulder • Framing a hind leg • Engaging a hind leg sideways

The position next to the inside hind leg is the standard position used at the Spanish Riding School for the walk and trot on a single track, as well as the shoulder-in. It allows the rider to use their own body to frame the inside hind leg and prevent it from escaping. As you can see, the rider's position with respect to the horse plays an important role in straightening, because it has a great influence over which legs can be framed.

The position of the reins also offers three basic variations:

- More or less horizontally along the side of the rib cage and pelvis
- Along the top of the croup or slightly off-centre across the croup muscle
- Diagonally across the back so that the right rein ends up next to the left hip, and vice versa

A rein that runs along the side of the horse is able to prevent the lateral hind leg from escaping sideways. It supports the turn as the outside rein, by directing the outside hind leg around the inside one. It can also frame and turn the rib cage when it is on the outside. As the inside rein it is able to drive the inside hind leg forwards-outwards in enlarging the circle and in the shoulder-in. In all these instances, the rein can always be supplemented with the whip.

If you rest the rein on top of the croup, it is possible to ask the hind leg to flex more during a half-halt by pressing down-wards with the edge of the hand. A releasing rein in this position opens the door for the lateral hind leg. This is often helpful in the early stages of long reining, when the horse does not yet stay on the first track very well.

If you run the outside rein along the top of the croup while using the inside rein horizontally along the horse's side, the horse will better understand that they are supposed to stay out on the first track. This method of holding the reins also helps in the early stages of the shoulder-in with many horses. When you put your hand on top of the croup, between the dock of the tail and the point of the hip, you can frame the hind leg on this side with your hand and the rein.

A rein that is run diagonally across the middle of the back frames the shoulder and is able either to frame the diagonal hind leg passively, or to engage it actively. When walking next to the inside hind leg in the shoulder-in, the outside rein guides the shoulders on to the inside track, while simultaneously framing the inside hind leg or engaging it with a nudge of the back of the hand if needed. In the haunches-in, renvers and half-pass, the inside rein runs across the middle of the back towards the outside. From this position it can ask for the lateral poll flexion and frame the inside shoulder, while also engaging the outside hind leg with a nudge of the back of the hand at the same time.

A nostalgic photo: Lipizzaner mare Sedonna was one of my early long rein horses and very important for my own development.
(Photo: Shana Ritter)

GETTING STARTED

Different Paths

The horse can be introduced to long reining in one of several different ways. One
logical approach is through double lungeing, by letting the horse go straight down
the long side of the arena while walking
behind them. I would recommend keeping
a larger distance from the hind legs initially, and closing it gradually. As soon as
you have come close enough to the horse
to touch the croup with your hands you no
longer need the lungeing surcingle, and
the two lunge lines can be replaced by
long reins.

The Portuguese type of work in hand,
where the trainer walks next to the horse's
shoulders, also offers a very convenient
introduction (see next section).

As an alternative, you can get behind
the horse and start to long rein right away,
while an assistant leads the horse with a
cavesson.

Portuguese-Style Work In-Hand

Over the years, I have tried all possible
variants of introducing horses to long reining. Every trainer will have his or her personal preferences. For me, Portuguese-
style work in-hand has been the most
effective; it does not require an assistant,
and it is safe for horse and rider. Besides,
you can explain many things to the horse
and develop a relationship of trust before
you walk directly behind them. It is also

PRE stallion Kabul on long reins, with Saskia Evertz as an assistant with the cavesson.

PRE stallion Kabul in the piaffe in-hand. The Portuguese work in-hand also offers a good way of introducing the horse to long reining. (Photos: Mader)

very well suited to developing the rider's skill in using the reins and the whip.

THE BEGINNING

The beginning is always hard. This applies to both work in-hand and long reining. You may have to struggle with the coordination of your hands and feet, and perhaps also with stamina. However, it is worthwhile persevering – the work gets easier over time, and it is fun to observe your own progress as well as that of the horse. Start by using the whole school. It is best to work in an arena with a solid kickboard, because the support of the wall helps a great deal in keeping the horse straight in the beginning. The rider stays next to the horse's shoulder. Hold the inside rein in your inside hand, and the outside rein together with the whip in your outside hand. The inside hand holds the rein rather short, directly behind the snaffle ring. You can even slip a finger through the snaffle ring. When you touch the horse's inside lower jaw with your inside hand, you can elevate him or flex the poll laterally, if necessary. With some horses it is advantageous to touch the lower neck with your inside hand, because you can elevate the neck, while framing the shoulder at the same time. For this position the rein has to be a little longer. The position of the hand and the rein length are determined by how and where you can help the horse most effectively.

THE POSITION OF THE OUTSIDE HAND

Many riders hold the outside hand somewhere around the middle of the rib cage. The advantage of this position is that the hind leg is within easier reach of the whip. On the downside, the inside shoulder is more difficult to frame, and the half-halts of the outside rein cannot connect as well with the outside hind leg if the horse pushes too much with the hind legs and does not carry enough owing to a lack of flexion of the haunches. The rider's elbow is then of necessity too far away from their body and too straight, which makes it difficult to establish a connection between the body weight, or the core muscles, and the hand.

Some riders hold their outside hand too high, almost on the outside of the withers. The resulting distance between elbow and hip quickly severs the connection between the core muscles and the hand, and the horse's shoulder can get pushed to the inside.

I prefer a position in which both my elbows are as close to my body as possible. The inside hand is close to the snaffle ring, and the outside one allows me to feel the horse's inside scapula. The whip should be long enough to be able to reach the hind legs.

The optimal posture can change from one stride to the next, in response to the horse's needs. One thing that does not change, however, is the fact that you need your core muscles for work in-hand. The rein contact, as well as the rein aids, must

Lipizzaner stallion Conversano Sorria with Shana Ritter. The rider's inside hand is holding the inside rein close to the snaffle ring. The outside hand is holding the outside rein and the whip. The outside hand is placed to frame the horse's inside shoulder. Simultaneously, it is able to control the horse's outside legs through the outside rein, while the whip can reach the inside hind leg. (Photo: Mader)

be anchored by and originate in the core muscles, for the reasons explained earlier.

TRANSITIONS IN-HAND

After the poll has been suppled laterally and longitudinally with flexion exercises, transitions between halt and walk are practised. The horse needs to learn to observe the rider's body language closely at first, starting to move as soon as the rid-er moves. You can make this clear to the

Core muscle engagement is necessary on long reins as well as for in-hand work. The rider's elbows must be kept as close to their body as possible for the rein aids to come through.

Portuguese style work in-hand is not only a good introduction to long reining, it is also helpful in teaching difficult movements. Friesian stallion Richold in piaffe. (Photo: Mader)

horse by facing backwards at the halt and facing forwards for the upward transition. Voice commands can also help in the beginning. Should the horse not move with the rider immediately, vibrate the whip against the inside hind leg or the spot on the rib cage where the rider's leg normally rests, until the horse starts to move.

The horse should get into habit of moving off with good energy from the very beginning. As in riding, it is the driving aids, in this case the whip, that bring the horse to the hand. A delayed reaction is an indication that the horse is inattentive and has fallen behind the aids, which always creates stiffness and resistances in other regions of the body, particularly the poll and hips.

The horse should stop in response to a light rein aid and the change in the rider's body language as soon as the rider stops and turns to face them. In the beginning, voice commands are also quite useful. Later on, they will generally not be necessary. This is the basic form of the exercise. As soon as the horse makes progress, it can be elaborated and refined.

CONTINUING WORK: TARGETED STOPS INTO THE INDIVIDUAL LEGS OF THE HORSE

The next step is to stop the horse from the walk into a specific leg. This is how it works. As always, the whip brings the horse to the hand, so they take a solid contact with the bit. The rider closes their fingers on the outside rein when the outside front leg is touching down. The full halt is executed in three strides, which means that you repeat your aid for three consecutive strides. The first two half-halts are preparatory aids, so the horse has time to prepare for the transition. The first two aids are therefore announcement commands, while the third is the execution command.

It is important here that the rein aids are supported by the rider's body weight, which should be directed into one foot that remains firmly on the ground during the half-halt. Should the horse offer to trot during the following up transition, we take

PRE stallion Kabul with Shana Ritter. The outside hand is placed further back. The inside hind leg can be reached more easily with the whip and the croup can be framed more effectively in this way. (Photo: Thomas Ritter)

it, but continue with the exercise otherwise unchanged. This means that halt-walk-halt transitions turn into halt-trot-halt transitions. Sometimes trot work is easier (at least for the horse) and more effective than work at the walk.

Once the outside front leg lets the half-halts go through, we turn to the outside hind leg. The walk-halt transitions are repeated with the outside rein when the outside hind leg is on the ground. Proceed in the same way as described above for the outside front leg.

Once the outside hind leg allows the half-halt to go through as well, we stop into the inside front leg. Now it is the inside rein that applies the half-halt when the inside front leg is on the ground. The final leg is the inside hind leg. The half-halt is applied with the inside rein again, just as for the inside front leg.

After addressing all four legs in this manner, change direction and repeat the entire sequence on the other rein.

As soon as the horse can execute transitions from walk to halt softly and smoothly, repeat the entire exercise sequence in the trot – should the horse not yet have offered the trot. This work is very suitable as a warm-up for horse and rider before mounted work. You can spend 10–15 minutes on it, before riding.

ANALYSING THE HORSE'S RESPONSES

Create a mental database of your horse's responses, and ask yourself the following questions: Which leg allowed the aids to go through best? Which leg showed the greatest resistance? Are the front legs more permeable than the hind legs, or vice versa? Is the outside pair of legs more accessible to the aids, or vice versa? Is one diagonal pair of legs more permeable than the other? The answers to these questions give us important insights into the current state of the horse's musculature, especially the poll, shoulders and hips.

COMMON PROBLEMS

Should the horse resist against the full halt, ask for flexion with the rein that asked for the downward transition, to explain to the horse that they are supposed to allow the aid to go through. The flexion should aim for the throatlatch area, while the neck should remain relatively straight. Straighten the horse after the flexion, and repeat flexing and straightening several times, until the horse softens at the throatlatch. As the lateral suppleness increases, the longitudinal flexion will also improve as a by-product of this exercise.

Should the horse try to evade by stepping back, ask them to take a step forward with each hind leg and repeat the flexion exercise. If the halt transition is not soft enough, ask the horse to walk on again, and repeat the downward transition at a different location in the arena.

If the backward evasion turns into a problem, the main focus becomes making sure the horse thinks forwards even at the halt and during the downward transition. The correction of this mistake is to trot on again and repeat the downward transition.

Horses with muscle blockages in the poll and neck often tend to run backwards, because their stiff neck muscles interrupt and deflect the thrust of the hindquarters backwards instead of allowing it to continue on to the bit. This often leads to a stiffening of the hips. Both muscle blockages support each other and it is often not clear where the vicious circle started. The solution usually requires alternating between suppling the poll and the hips with appropriate exercises. Some of these types of stiffness can be resolved more effectively under saddle, others through flexion in-hand, and some can be resolved on the long rein itself.

EXERCISE: VARY THE STRIDE LENGTH

Once the transitions are established, it is time to build on what the horse has learned so far. The horse should now learn to lengthen the stride at the trot when the rider walks faster, so that the horse never leaves the trainer's side. For this purpose, the rider increases the pressure of the hind legs against the ground with a vibration of the whip against the haunches or the rib cage, which is then released into longer strides by carefully giving with the reins as the rider walks faster. Later on, the horse should push forward spontaneously when the rider accelerates.

The rider should stay at the walk as much as possible during this exercise,

The horse must be in front of the leg (or the whip, respectively) and think forwards at all times.

even though the horse is trotting, to avoid losing the connection to the ground that allows the rein aids to go through. If the rider starts jogging, their movement will interfere with the rein contact. Moreover, an unintentional yank on the rein could be interpreted as a punishment by the horse and take away their desire to go forwards.

When the rider slows down again, the horse is supposed to collect and to shorten the stride. In order to prevent the horse from sucking back, it is often necessary to increase the energy level with a vibration of the whip. This energy needs to be transformed into shorter strides with half-halts into a foreleg or a hind leg. Initially, relatively small, incremental changes in stride length will suffice. Later on, this can be developed into trot - piaffe - trot transitions. The goal is to keep horse and trainer together at all times, regardless of whether the gait is fast or slow.

EXERCISE: CHANGE RIDER POSITION BY VARYING THE STRIDE LENGTH

An exercise that can be introduced at this point involves asking the horse to lengthen

Lipizzaner stallion Maestoso II Shama II. The rider should remain at the walk as much as possible, even when the horse is trotting or cantering. (Photo: Mader)

and shorten the stride while the rider maintains the same speed. This means that the horse will pass the rider for a few strides, while the rider drops back from the horse's shoulder to the rib cage, and from there to the horse's hips. The rider then shortens the horse's stride and catches up to regain the original position next to the shoulder.

Relatively small differences in stride length are sufficient in the beginning. Later, the rider can ask the horse to lengthen the stride to medium or even extended trot and allow them to increase the distance until the end of the long rein has been reached. Sooner or later, the rider has to

The rider remains at the walk as much as possible, even when the horse is trotting or cantering.

start running with the horse because the speed of the trot is too fast, even with smaller horses. Include this exercise in the workout from time to time to check whether the horse is still honestly in front of the whip.

This exercise is for the rider's benefit. The horse continues to trot at the same tempo and stride length, while the rider slows down for a few strides. When the rider arrives next to the hind legs, they speed up again until they are next to the shoulders. The horse's gait and posture must not change throughout. The challenge for the rider is to cover a relatively large distance without losing the rein contact or disturbing the horse. In other words, you have to let a very long piece of rein slip through your fingers, and then shorten it again without losing the connection or getting stuck.

Long Reining with an Assistant

Working with an assistant makes it easier to keep the horse on the outside track, which often presents the greatest challenge in the beginning, especially on the stiffer side. Attach the long rein to the snaffle rings. An assistant frames the horse with the help of a lead rein, attached to the

centre ring of the cavesson, and a whip. Should the horse suck back and hesitate to go forwards, the assistant can ask them to go forwards with gentle tugs on the lead rein and with vibrations of the whip on the side of the rib cage or the haunches. As long as the horse is moving forwards at the walk or trot, the assistant merely ensures that they stay on the wall. As the work progresses, the assistant becomes more and more passive, assuming the function of a second wall, while the trainer guides the horse from behind.

Once the work has progressed to the point where the horse is moving forwards and staying on the outside track without help, the trainer can continue without the assistant and start practising the halt transitions into individual legs as described above.

In order to preserve the desire to go forwards, one should continue to practise lengthening the strides at the trot. An important goal of the upward and downward transitions is to create a sufficiently strong urge to go forward in the horse that they will start moving their legs forwards at the slightest release of the reins, without any additional driving aids.

Sequences of Transitions

Transitions should be revisited frequently throughout training. I want to give an example of how transitions can be made

PRE stallion Kabul with Saskia Evertz assisting with the cavesson. This is an easy and convenient way to introduce long reining to an inexperienced horse. (Photo: Mader)

more sophisticated for the more advanced horse by riding them in sequences. Once the horse has learned to execute simple transitions and to stop into individual legs, you can connect two legs with each other in the downward transition by connecting them to the rein and the ground, as explained above. For instance, you can ride a transition from trot to walk or to halt by connecting the front legs with each other. A suitable sequence would be: outside – inside – outside.

Three aids are spread out over three steps. "Outside - inside - outside" is a short form for a half-halt on the outside rein when the outside front leg is on the ground. This is followed by the inside rein applying a half-halt when the inside fore-leg is on the ground, and finally the outside rein half-halts again when the outside front leg is grounded. This final half-halt stops the horse.

After this, ask the horse to trot on and turn your attention to another pair of

PRE stallion Amigo with Andreas Evertz. (Photo: Shana Ritter)

legs, for example the hind legs. These could be connected with each other through the sequence inside - outside - inside.

This asks for a half-halt with the inside rein when the inside hind leg is on the ground. The second half-halt is applied with the outside rein when the outside hind leg is on the ground, and the third half-halt stops the horse into the inside hind leg with the inside rein.

Afterwards the trot is resumed and the outside pair of legs is connected with each other. You could choose the sequence of front – rear – front for this.

The fourth sequence could connect the inside pair of legs with each other, with the sequence rear – front – rear.

The fifth exercise in the series could connect the legs of the main diagonal with each other through the sequence: inside rear – outside front – inside rear.

The final exercise in this context connects the legs of the secondary diagonal through the sequence: outside rear – inside front – outside rear.

GET CREATIVE

This exercise is only one of many possibilities. The legs can be connected with each other in many different ways. I would like to encourage you to experiment with these ideas! As soon as the transitions described above succeed smoothly, you can start practising the same sequences of rein aids at the trot, but this time without changing gait or stride length. Another evolution of the exercise consists of almost stopping with these rein aid sequences, and then continuing the trot at the last second. The goal is to maintain the same tempo (strides per minute), but to shorten the stride length so the horse trots almost on the spot for one to three strides and continues forward with the fourth stride. This is one potential path towards the piaffe (see section on the piaffe). Once the horse is able to execute three strides almost on the spot

Exercises:

- *Connect the front legs with each other through half-halts: outside — inside — outside*

- *Connect the hind legs with each other through half-halts: inside — outside — inside*

- *Connect the outside pair of legs with each other through half-halts: front — rear — front*

- *Connect the inside pair of legs with each other through half-halts: rear — front — rear*

- *Connect the legs of the main diagonal with each other through half-halts: inside rear — outside front — inside rear*

- *Connect the legs of the secondary diagonal with each other through half-halts: outside rear — inside front — outside rear*

without losing tempo or impulsion, the number of these strides can be increased to five, then seven, and so on.

The demands can be further increased by practising all the transitions described above in the lateral movements as well. The shoulder-in is the first to attempt. When the horse has mastered the transitions in shoulder-in, the same exercises can be tried in all the other lateral movements. If one hind leg shows a great deal of resistance, you should choose sequences that end with this particular hind leg so that the transition is executed into this leg.

The rein aids must go through in these exercises without the "engine" stalling. The horse should continue with redoubled effort afterwards, like a rubber ball that bounces even higher after hitting the ground.

Lipizzaner stallion Maestoso II Shama II. Get creative in connecting the horse's legs with each other through half-halts. (Photo: Mader)

More energy must not lead to tension or to quicker steps. Conversely, slowing down or shortening the strides must not cause a loss of impulsion. By the same token, increasing suppleness must not create a loss of impulsion. So it is not a choice between impulsion and relaxation, but both at the same time! And not a choice between impulsion and collection, but both at the same time!

Training Duration

As far as the duration of the training and the sequence of the training steps is concerned, there are no hard and fast rules. As a general rule, horses learn faster than their riders. That is why training the first horse takes the longest. Once the rider knows how to do it and has mastered the subject matter in theory and in practice, the duration of the training process may be considerably shorter with the following horses. The training time in long reining is also greatly influenced by the amount of training the horse has received previously. For example, a horse that has been trained to Grand Prix under saddle merely has to be introduced to the specific long rein aids, which can be done in a few months. If you start with a Second Level horse by comparison, several years of training will be required before the horse can produce the most difficult movements.

However, as a general rule, the old principle holds that the duration of the training process is determined by the horse. Horse training is mainly work on the basics. Establishing the correct basics enables the horse to perform correct movements. The highest priority is, therefore, that the horse remains honestly in front of the driving aids and that they become more permeable and supple during training. Flexibility and self-carriage are the cornerstones of dressage here as well. On this foundation, it is possible to build higher equestrian art. Should problems arise in certain dressage movements, the root cause will always lie in deficiencies in the basics, such as balance, suppleness, straightness and permeability. Therefore, every correction must begin with an improvement of the basics. Otherwise, the horse is being trick trained instead of educated. The importance of revisiting the basics regularly cannot be emphasised enough – even, and especially, with advanced horses. Trotting and cantering straight ahead on a single track, on the bit, with transitions between the gaits, should

PRE stallion Amigo with Andreas Evertz in the piaffe on long reins, with the support of a second trainer with the cavesson and whip. (Photo: Shana Ritter)

be a regular part of every training session. Turning and bending in motion, as well as flexions at the halt, should also be practised regularly.

The Sequence of the Training Steps

There are certain rules of thumb that can be established for the sequence in which the different training topics are introduced. They will work for the majority of cases. They must not, however, be regarded as set in stone. Each horse is different.

In my practical experience it has worked well to use the whole school at the walk and trot at the beginning of training, and practise transitions between halt, walk, and trot with correctly executed corners.

The next training period includes the circle, 90-degree turns away from the long side of the arena, as well as shoulder-in and haunches-in on the long side. It is recommended that less experienced riders begin with the circle and turning away from the arena wall before attempting lateral movements, just as under saddle. Experienced trainers can afford to handle the sequence flexibly.

Half-passes are traditionally introduced after the shoulder-in and haunches-in on the long side. Canter work begins as soon as the horse starts to offer the first canter strides. If a horse lacks talent in the canter, one should postpone the canter work until after they have learned to perform haunches-in, renvers and half-passes at the trot.

The piaffe can be started in-hand relatively early. This training runs parallel to the work on long reins. As soon as the horse piaffes well in-hand, the skill can be transferred to the long rein.

The passage should generally be introduced after the piaffe. But, as always, experienced trainers can afford to make exceptions. The levade develops out of the piaffe.

Highly collected movements such as the piaffe, passage, canter pirouettes and levade can easily cause tightness in the abdominal muscles and a degree of lateral bracing of the horse's hips. It is therefore important to return to voltes, circles, figure eights and lateral movements in order to supple these muscles again.

Next page: Evi Petrak in the correct posture with the Austrian warmblood mare Bellissima. (Photo: Schneider)

Lipizzaner stallion Maestoso II Shama II demonstrating the shoulder-in. Engaged core muscles and straight rider posture are prerequisites for the horse's self-carriage. (Photo: Shana Ritter)

COMMON MISTAKES

The Rider's Gait and Posture

As far as the rider's posture, stride length, and gait are concerned, there are a few common mistakes that happen especially during the early stages of long reining.

INSUFFICIENT CORE MUSCLE ENGAGEMENT

Many riders do not engage their core muscles enough, so that their shoulders tip forward (duck butt!). This causes the horse to get strung out and drag their feet. The horse reacts to driving aids by walking faster and falling apart even more, instead of collecting and elevating.

It is extremely important that the rider walks upright in good posture, with the shoulders vertically above the pelvis, and with well engaged core muscles. This enables them to activate the horse with their own physical energy alone and to "push" the horse before them.

JIGGING RIDER

Another common mistake consists in taking quick, tiny steps and more or less jogging behind the horse in the hope that the horse will start trotting someday. This

Conversano Sorria at the trot in-hand. Should the horse suck back behind the aids, the best correction is to move next to the horse's shoulder and revisit the transitions. (Photo: Shana Ritter)

is another case of insufficient core muscle engagement, and the horse will generally remain strung out and without energy. Instead, one should try from the beginning to take long strides from the hips and to remain at the walk as much as possible even if the horse is trotting or cantering. This takes some practice, but it makes the aids considerably more effective.

STEPPING ON THE HORSE'S HEELS

During the early stages of long reining, in particular, it is common for the rider to step on the horse's heels when walking close behind the horse. The reason is that the horse is not yet engaging the hind legs enough. As soon as the haunches become more active and engage more underneath the centre of gravity, the perceived "space issue" of the rider's feet will disappear.

Undesirable Reactions by the Horse

Especially during the introduction to long reining, the horse will not always respond as desired. Here are some typical mistakes and their corrections.

SUCKING BACK

A sucked-back horse poses a potentially mortal danger, especially if they carry their head low and croup high, because the danger of kicking out is very great. This is why sucking back is not addressed from behind the horse for safety reasons.

There are several possible ways to deal successfully with this issue. I would start out by stepping next to the horse's shoulder and revisiting the transitions between walk and trot, insisting on an impulsive transition into the trot.

This approach should draw the horse out again. If the problem is more deeply rooted, it is more effective to lunge correctly. You can go forwards on the long side, so that the horse lengthens the stride in the trot. The sucked-back horse will break into a canter at first, or even start bucking. In this case, return to a circle, bring the horse back into a calm but energetic trot, and then try lengthening the strides down the long side again. This is repeated until the horse lengthens the strides without breaking into a canter or bucking. In addition, it is necessary to get the horse in front of the leg under saddle.

LACK OF REIN CONTACT

Many novices walk with too little rein contact and allow the horse to move along with their nose almost on the ground. As soon as the rider engages their core muscles and activates the horse's hindquarters, the horse will approach the hand more so that the reins can be shortened and the frame becomes more compact from back to front.

LEAVING THE TRACK

It is common for the horse not to stay on the track on their stiff side, but instead to drift to the inside. The reason for this is crookedness, of course. Here the rider needs to check their position and framing aids (see the paragraph on framing rein aids).

CURLING UP

Many horses curl up. This is especially common with "swan-necked" horses. The cause is that the hindquarters are not working actively enough and not engaging under the centre of gravity, and flexion of the haunches is lacking.

The correction involves asking the hindquarters to become livelier and engage more and, secondly, flexing the haunches through half-halts (see the paragraph on half-halts). This is potentially more effective in the shoulder-in than on a single track.

Sometimes it is necessary to step next to the shoulder again and to practise a few

Lipizzaner stallion Maestoso II Shama II showing correct rein contact and great impulsion from the hindquarters. (Photo: Shana Ritter)

transitions from the walk or halt into an active working trot.

If the loss of elevation is only small and brief, the rider can show the horse the way uphill with their hands. The old principle always applies, however, that the driving aids first have to bring the horse to the hand. If the problem is more deeply rooted or more pronounced, the only recourse is to return to the basics.

HIGH CROUP, STIFF HAUNCHES

Some horses push the croup up, especially in the canter, and carry themselves on their forehand. This happens especially easily in long reining, because the rider cannot use their own body weight to load and flex the hindquarters. In this case it is sometimes helpful to put both reins on top of the horse's croup and to press vertically down onto the croup. In addition, the rider can try to support and increase the lifting of the withers with one of the reins during the first beat of the canter stride, when the outside hind leg is on the ground. It is generally not sufficient to correct the canter on long reins alone – it will be necessary to improve it under saddle as well.

HORSE ABOVE THE BIT

Horses whose neck conformation is less than ideal are often not easy to get on the bit because the distance between the hand and the bit is very large. Flexions at the halt with the rider standing in front of the horse or next to the head will help here. In this way, the rider can gently supple the stiff muscles, which mobilizes the poll and improves the rein contact. Portuguese-style work in-hand will prove to be useful as well.

PRE gelding Furia with Andreas Evertz. Riding correctly using the whole school is the prerequisite for all other arena patterns (Photo: Shana Ritter)

Thomas Ritter is turning Lipizzaner stallion Conversano Sorria on to a volte in the canter. (Photo: Maresa Mader)

FIRST ARENA PATTERNS

From the Corner to the Serpentine

The early stages of long reining are usually done around the whole school, until the horse goes straight and forwards without sucking back and without drifting away from the wall. Since the riding arena has four corners, the rider is confronted with the task of bending the horse and turning the corner four times during each lap around the arena, which is more difficult on long reins than under saddle. Once this exercise succeeds, changes of direction and other curved lines are added.

Corners

Almost all horses try to cut the corners, moving around an oval track without bending. If the rider permits this, the horse becomes stiffer and stiffer, especially on the inside. It is therefore important to study the concept of correctly-ridden corners on long reins, because in many ways corners are the gateway to curved lines and lateral movements. The corner is a key element in gymnastic horse training.

The corner should be executed in three strides of the inside hind leg, because this is the smallest circle which the horse can describe on a single track. If the horse takes

The corner is the gateway to curved lines and lateral movements, which makes it a key element of gymnastic horse training.

Corners represent a challenge on long reins because horses often do not bend enough and deviate from the line to the inside. Given that weight and leg aids are not available it is more difficult to insist on a correct execution. It is well worth the effort, however, as those who are able to ride correct corners have fewer problems with higher level movements later.

the corner in more strides, they will fall onto the inside shoulder, cut the corner and ignore the inside aids.

Full-pass into the corner.

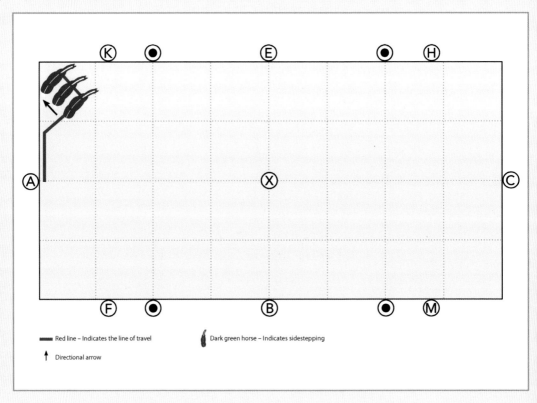

Red line – Indicates the line of travel

Dark green horse – Indicates sidestepping

Directional arrow

In a large arena, it takes a long time to get from one corner to the next. The distance between the corners can be shortened by riding a 90 degree turn away from the long side 20m after the corner. Ride across the width of the arena, parallel to the short side, and turn in the same direction on the opposite long side. Follow the long side for 10m, turn again through 90 degrees, ride across the width of the arena, parallel to the short side, and turn in the same direction on the opposite long side. Follow the long side for 20m, and turn again. This creates 10mx20m rectangles that "migrate" from one short side to the other.

The distance between the corners can be shortened by riding smaller rectangles.

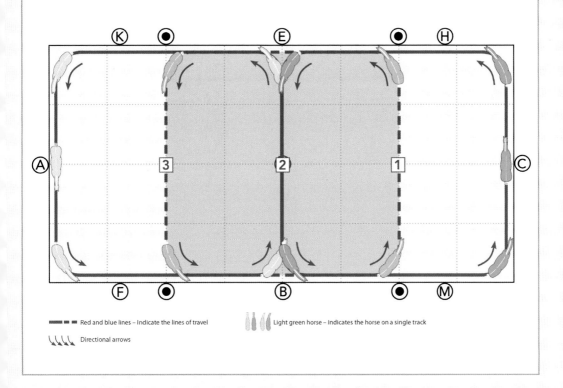

━ ■ ■ Red and blue lines – Indicate the lines of travel

◝◝◝ Directional arrows

ᶦᶦᶦ ᶦᶦᶦ Light green horse – Indicates the horse on a single track

It has proven helpful to walk between the wall and the outside hind leg in the corner and to push the inside hind leg out with the inside rein and whip, as in a leg yield. The rider can think of shoulder-in or enlarging the circle. The whip is held in the inside hand and either presses horizontally against the horse's rib cage or touches the inside hind leg as it is swinging forward. The more the inside hind leg engages underneath the centre of the body, the better the horse will bend laterally. The inside rein can run along the inside hind leg between the stifle and the point of the hip. The outside rein makes room for the horse, either by opening slightly towards the outside or running along the top of the croup, which works better if the rider is walking directly behind the horse.

The position between the croup and the wall works well with horses who have a strong tendency to cut the corner and ignore the inside aids. In extreme cases, it helps to stop in the middle of the corner and execute a full-pass toward the wall. The sudden interruption of the flow of the work draws the horse's attention to the aids, which they had been ignoring. The following exercise then explains to the horse how they should have reacted.

The position behind the horse is the next training step, once the horse has learned to yield to the inside aids.

Finally, it is possible to walk next to the inside hind leg without the horse cutting the corner, escaping to the outside with the haunches, or giving up the bend. This may sound simple, but it requires a fairly high level of training.

Circles and Voltes

The aids for circles and voltes are very similar to the aids for corners. In the beginning it will probably be easiest to walk next to the outside hind leg. The disadvantage of this approach is that the rider has to cover a greater distance than the horse, which means they have to walk faster than the trotting or cantering horse. The advantage of the outside track is that the horse can be framed very effectively between the rider's body, the inside rein, and the whip. The circle of aids can be established very easily by enlarging the circle. The whip and inside rein drive the inside hind leg forwards - outwards while the rider's body frames the outside hind leg, and the outside rein receives the impulse of the inside hind leg. The inside rein can bend the horse. The bending rein aid can be applied, as already mentioned, when the lateral front leg has touched down or when the lateral hind leg is on the ground. It works best when the inside rein touches the rib cage and the inside hip (see the section on bending rein aids).

As soon as the horse maintains the line of the circle or volte well, you can walk behind the croup, so that you are walking on the same track as the horse. How the reins are held depends on the horse's current needs. A rein that runs along the top of the croup allows the horse to stretch this side of the body or to yield with the croup toward this side. A rein that runs diagonally across the back can easily push the croup in the opposite direction where the frame is now lacking.

With a highly advanced horse you can also walk on the inside without the haunches escaping towards the outside.

Serpentines and Rectangles

Among the most difficult exercises on long reins are serpentines and rectangles. For the sake of precision, serpentines should be ridden so that the loops consist of semicircles that touch the long side for one stride and that connect to each other through straight lines. These straight lines run parallel to the short side. This gives

Serpentines in four loops.

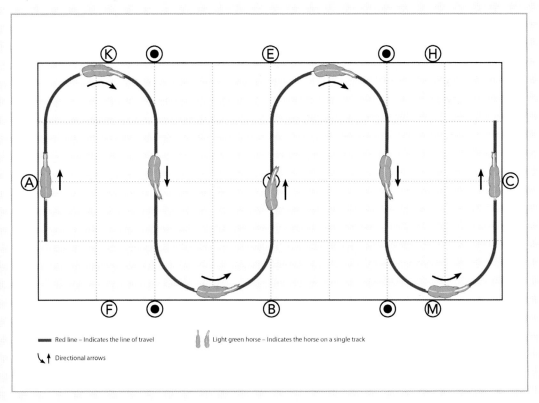

Red line – Indicates the line of travel   Light green horse – Indicates the horse on a single track

Directional arrows

Lipizzaner stallion Conversano Sorria executing a turn. In turns, the inside rein sends the horse into the outside rein, which then turns the shoulder. Thus, the inside rein takes on the job of the inside leg under saddle. (Photo: Mader)

you excellent reference points to check the correctness of the execution.

The bend is changed when crossing the centre line. In practical terms, this means the change of bend needs to be prepared when leaving the long side. In order to change direction and maintain good balance, it is necessary to establish the new bend before turning in the new direction. Otherwise, the horse will fall onto the new inside shoulder and lose their balance.

Many horses invert in the transition from the turn to the straight line towards the opposite long side. The challenge consists in not letting the horse get crooked, in order to avoid this. The exercise succeeds best when the horse can be "pushed" back and forth between the reins. During the first half of the serpentine loop, think of enlarging the circle. The horse should yield to the inside rein, bend towards the inside and stretch into the outside rein.

The outside rein receives the horse and turns him, so they do not simply follow the wall. This rein becomes the inside one, and with a slight lateral pressure brings the horse into the new outside rein, which then begins the next loop in the other direction. Lowering the outside rein a little in the beginning makes turns easier, because this increases its lateral driving effect. In this way, the inside rein always brings the horse into the outside one. The outside rein receives the horse and brings them back into the inside one, etc.

The big challenge for the rider is to move from one side of the horse to the other without interfering with the rein contact each time. This is not easy in the beginning, and can only be learned through a lot of practice.

Another good exercise is a kind of serpentine with corners: leave the wall at a 90 degree angle as in a corner and ride straight across to the opposite long side. There, turn through 90 degrees again in the opposite direction, and continue in this way until you have gone from A to C or vice versa.

Straight Lines without the Support of the Arena Wall

Just as under saddle, you should practise long reining on straight lines at a certain distance from the wall. It is important the horse is aligned straight on the line of travel and that the distance to the wall does not change. Many horses gradually reduce the distance, because they drift closer to the security of the wall. This is most pronounced in the canter, because the canter posture has a certain affinity to the haunches-in and the rider can easily lose control of the outside shoulder or the inside hind leg.

Working on the third track or the quarter line, straightness can be controlled most effectively by walking directly behind the horse. In this position, any deviation can be noticed and corrected immediately.

Should the horse drift back towards the wall, the outside rein is run low along the outside of the horse; the whip drives the outside hind leg forward, and may press against the outside of the rib cage until the horse is straight again.

The problems described here all occur under saddle as well. On long reins they are much more visible, however – almost as if under a magnifying glass – because the rider's options are more limited.

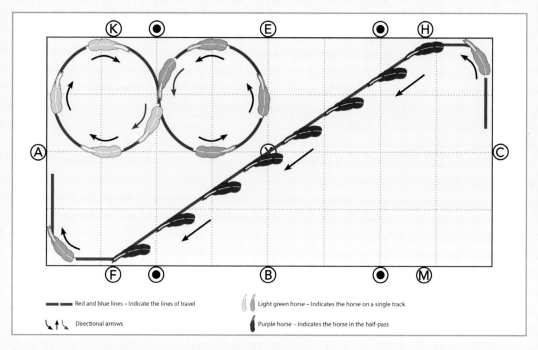

Half passes and figures of eight are good options for changing rein.

Changing direction by reversing into the corner and out of the corner.

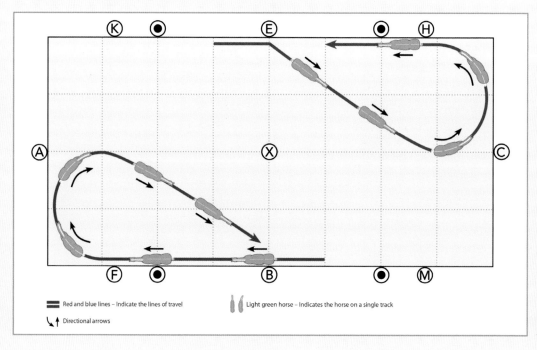

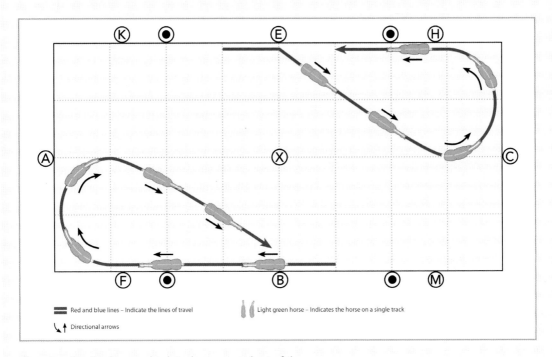

Red and blue lines – Indicate the lines of travel

Light green horse – Indicates the horse on a single track

Directional arrows

Changing direction by reversing into the corner and out of the corner.

Changing Direction

On long reins you can change direction through arena patterns, turns on the haunches, passades or pirouettes. The turn on the forehand is not practised.

The aids for the arena patterns can be derived from the descriptions of corners, voltes, circles, serpentines and straight lines in the previous sections. Turns on the haunches, passades and pirouettes will be described in the following chapter on the movements.

Lipizzaner stallion Maestoso II Shama II in the levade. (Photo: Mader)

THE MOVEMENTS

(Almost) Anything is Possible

Almost all dressage movements can be trained on long reins – even zigzag half-passes and pirouettes. Medium and extended gaits are usually not shown, however, although lengthening the strides in the trot from time to time can help to refresh the gait and keep the horse in front of the aids. As long as the rider can keep up with the horse, transitions within the gait are quite useful, because otherwise the gaits can become dull and stiff. Complementary work under saddle is very important to keep the horse in front of the aids and to prevent stiffness.

The Lateral Movements

As soon as the horse is able to go on the bit in the walk and trot on a single track, it is time to start lateral work. Shoulder-in should be practised first, followed by haunches-in and half-passes.

Half-passes from the centre line to the middle of the long side of the arena are generally easier for horse and rider than half-passes on the diagonals. Therefore, it makes sense to begin with half-passes from the centre line.

Renvers can be introduced at the same time as the haunches-in. When shoulder-in and haunches-in succeed reasonably well, one should begin practising turns on the haunches.

RIB CAGE BENDING AS A PREREQUISITE

Riding correctly through the corner (see the section on corners) is the prerequisite for successful lateral movements. If the horse does not bend well in the corner, the lateral work will fail, because lateral bending is the most crucial feature of correct lateral movements. Without the rib cage bend, the horse may be moving sideways but at least one hind leg is no longer stepping underneath the centre of gravity and escaping sideways. The exercise consequently loses its gymnastic value, because the escaping hind leg is out of reach of the rider's influence and can no longer be flexed. It starts to brace and can become the starting point of disobedience. As Gustav Steinbrecht (1885) explained: "It is only the rib cage bend that enables the horse to direct the thrust of his hind legs undiminished towards his forehand in the lateral movements, because the hind legs of the bending horse are able to engage underneath the body mass in these movements, whereas the hind legs of the horse that does not bend must step past the load if the sideways movement is to continue. Correct movements on two tracks are therefore unthinkable without rib cage bending, and a lack thereof will show up as a drifting croup and an interruption of the gait, as well as through a poor rein contact."

Should the corner be executed poorly it is better not to even start the lateral movement but to ride a volte in the corner first, in order to establish the lateral bend. If one volte is not enough, it can be repeated until the necessary bend is there. The rib cage bend can be recreated most easily by walking next to the outside hind leg and pushing the inside hind leg forwards-outwards with the inside rein and the whip in the direction of the outside shoulder.

Lipizzaner stallion Conversano Sorria. In shoulder-in the horse is positioned as in the first stride of a volte. (Photo: Mader)

The inside rein bends the horse in the throatlatch and the neck. The outside rein makes room for the croup by running along the middle of the croup. Simultaneously, it frames the outside shoulder.

The rib cage bend is the same in the lateral movements as in corners and voltes. Corners and voltes are therefore the gymnastic precursors, the steps on the training ladder that have to be climbed before attempting lateral movements. Once the rib cage bend is established, you only need to leave the corner or volte, and the door to the lateral movements is open. In the shoulder-in, the horse is positioned as in the first stride of the volte. In the haunches-in, they are positioned as in the last step of the volte.

SHOULDER-IN

I usually begin the shoulder-in out of a corner, or sometimes out of a volte.

The horse should bend well and engage the inside hind leg far underneath the body without the outside hind leg escaping towards the outside. The more the outside hind leg supports the weight and flexes its upper joints, the more the inside hind leg can engage underneath the centre of gravity.

THE AIDS

The preparation for a shoulder-in on the long side involves the two corners of the preceding short side. Bringing the horse into a shoulder-in position is easiest for beginners when they turn their own pelvis slightly to assume a shoulder-in position themselves, by rotating their outside hip and shoulder forwards. The outside rein yields automatically and the inside rein is shortened a little as a result. If the horse has stretched well into the outside rein beforehand, they will immediately follow the yielding outside rein by bringing the outside shoulder forward.

Lipizzaner stallion Conversano Sorria. In haunches-in the horse is positioned as in the last stride of a volte. (Photo: Mader)

> *With good preparation of the movement you are already half way there.*

As soon as the horse assumes the shoulder-in position, the outside rein catches them again, so they do not drift away from the wall to the inside of the are-na. The horse should have learned at this point to respond to a light lateral pressure against the hip by sidestepping. The whip can be applied either on the inside of the rib cage, on the inside hind leg or on the outside of the rib cage. Applied on the inside, it supports the bend and the engagement of the inside hind leg, and prevents the horse from drifting in. Touching the outside of the rib cage, it helps bring the shoulder to the inside. Touching the out-

Lipizzaner stallion Conversano Sorria in a shoulder-in at the trot. The outside rein is running along the middle of the croup here. This enables the rider to frame the outside shoulder well and to create the necessary opening for the horse's outside hip to move forward. The inside rein gently squeezes the inside hind leg underneath the horse's body. (Photo: Mader)

side hind leg asks it to step forward instead of escaping towards the outside.

Depending on the horse's level of training and the individual situation, the rider can walk either next to the outside hind leg, directly behind the croup or next to the inside hind leg. Between the outside hind leg and the wall is the best position for preventing the horse from drifting to the inside. The inside rein is placed between the inside stifle and hip. The outside rein can be opened a little to create a clear space for the horse to fill with their body.

Soft bending aids with the inside rein create and maintain the softness of the inner side. They are most effective when the inside front leg is on the ground. Afterwards they are repeated for the inside hind leg.

When I walk behind the horse, I like to put the outside rein on top of the outer half of the croup or directly on the middle of the croup, which allows me to frame the out-

Lipizzaner stallion Maestoso II Shama II in a correct shoulder-in. (Photo: Shana Ritter)

side shoulder and flex the outside hind leg at the same time.

With very advanced horses (or on a horse's hollow side) you can move next to the inside hind leg as well. The outside rein then runs across the middle of the back to turn the outside shoulder. The inside rein can be opened a little to improve the bend, if necessary.

MISTAKES AND CORRECTIONS

There are three main mistakes in the shoulder-in:

- The horse leaves the wall and drifts to the inside. Walk on the outside of the croup and bring the horse towards you with the inside rein.
- The horse escapes toward the outside with his outside hind leg and bends to the outside, creating an incorrect renvers. Walk next to the outside hind leg and work on establishing the correct bend with the inside rein and the whip on the inside, while framing the outside hind leg with your own body.
- The horse overbends the neck to the inside while sticking to the wall with their shoulder. Either walk next to the inside hind leg and guide the shoulder towards the inside with the outside rein or walk behind the horse and bring the shoulder inwards with a combination of outside rein and the whip touching on the outside of the horse's body, which lets the outside hind leg step further forward.

SHOULDER-IN ON THE CIRCLE

The shoulder-in should be practised on the circle to improve the lateral bend. The rider usually walks slightly to the outside of the horse and squeezes the inside hind leg with the inside rein and the whip forwards – outwards. The outside rein either opens a little towards the outside, or it is placed on top of the croup so the horse understands that there is an open space on the outside when they yield to the inside aids. This exercise brings the horse nicely into the outside rein and prepares the canter.

SPIRALLING IN AND OUT ON THE CIRCLE

A good variation on the shoulder-in on the circle is to spiral in and out. Spiralling in can be ridden in a haunches-in position; spiralling out is related to shoulder-in. This exercise is a very good preparation for the canter and the pirouettes. In spiralling in, the challenge lies in controlling the inside hind leg so the horse does not simply run sideways nor get behind the aids. The rider keeps the inside rein ready to catch the inside hind leg and send it forward again. It should therefore not be moved too far to the outside if the horse has a tendency to swing the haunches too far in.

When spiralling in on a single track, the smallest volte is executed in 12 strides of the inside hind leg. If you want to decrease the size of the volte further, you have to give the horse a haunches-in position,

Lipizzaner stallion Maestoso II Shama II in the canter pirouette. Spiralling in on the circle is a good preparation. (Photo: Mader)

turning the volte into a passade, which can then be decreased into a pirouette.

When spiralling out, the horse must not drift to the outside with the outside shoulder. The hips and shoulders should step forwards and outwards at the same rate. Therefore, the inside rein touches the side of the inside hip, while the outside rein runs along the middle of the croup. The inside rein is then able to squeeze the inside hind leg forwards – outwards, and the outside rein frames the outside shoulder.

Just as in riding, the diagonal pairs of legs are connected with each other to straighten the horse. The inside hind leg (inside leg aid) and outside front leg (outside rein) play an especially important role in this.

The Austrian warmblood mare Bayenne with Evi Petrak, performing the haunches-in. (Photo: Schneider)

THE HAUNCHES-IN

The haunches-in shares the bend to the inside of the arena with the shoulder-in. The difference is that the horse is bent in the direction of travel in the haunches-in, so the outside legs step in front of the inside legs, whereas the horse is bent against the direction of travel in the shoulder-in so the inside legs step in front of the outside legs. Another difference is that in the

haunches-in the front legs stay on the first track while the hind legs are moved to the inside. In the shoulder-in the opposite occurs. The hindquarters stay on the first track while the shoulders are moved to the inside.

THE AIDS

In some ways, the haunches-in on the long side is easier to obtain than the shoulder-in. The rider only needs to step next to the outside hind leg and run the inside rein across the middle of the back to the outside, so their inside hand ends up next to the horse's outside hind leg. Some horses will assume the haunches-in position on their own as a result. Should this not be the case, you can push the haunches away from the wall with the back of your inside hand. This aid is applied at the moment when the outside hind leg is in the air.

The inside rein can half-halt gently at the same time to flex the throatlatch laterally and the inside hind leg longitudinally. It can also remain passive while the outside rein is shortened slightly. The outside rein aid utilises the lateral leverage of the horse's neck to let the croup yield in the opposite direction. In practice you will often have to support the yielding of the croup with the outside rein first, and then improve the bend with the inside rein afterwards. The rider must feel which aid is needed at any given time in order to make the horse's job easier.

MISTAKES AND CORRECTIONS

A typical mistake in the haunches-in is that the angle between the horse's body and the line of travel becomes too steep, because the haunches are escaping to the inside and the horse is no longer going forwards enough. Often the bend is lost. The correction is to move directly behind the horse, place the inside rein on top of the inside half of the croup and drive the inside hind leg straight forward with the whip. It may be necessary to change one's position and the aids again after a few strides.

This mistake and others can be avoided by not staying in one lateral movement for too long but transitioning into another lateral movement after a few strides. Shoulder-in and haunches-in complement each other very well in this respect. The shoulder-in engages the inside hind leg under the body mass if it has escaped to the inside in the haunches-in. The haunches-in brings the outside hind leg back

Lipizzaner stallion Conversano Sorria with Shana Ritter in the shoulder-in. (Photo: Mader)

Lipizzaner stallion Conversano Sorria with Shana Ritter in the haunches-in. (Photo: Mader)

under the body if it has escaped to the outside in the shoulder-in.

As an alternative, you can turn onto a volte out of the haunches-in. The volte also requires sending the inside hind leg forward underneath the body first, before the outside shoulder can be turned. With this exercise you can prevent a loss of control over the inside hind leg and the outside front leg.

Pay close attention to the lateral bend in the haunches-in – as you should in all lateral movements. The horse must not merely march sideways with his inside hind leg, but also step forward underneath the body mass and assume a soft, supple lateral bend. The rib cage bend and the engagement and flexion of the inside hind leg are mutually dependent. One is not possible without the other. If the horse loses the lateral bend and the flexion of the inside hind leg, the haunches-in loses its gymnastic value and one is left with an unintentional leg yield.

PRE stallion Amigo with Andreas Evertz in the renvers. (Photo: Shana Ritter)

RENVERS

In the renvers, the croup remains on the first track while the shoulders are moved to the inside, as in the shoulder-in. The difference is that the horse is bent against the direction of travel in the shoulder-in so that the inside legs step in front of the outside legs. The renvers can therefore be developed simply by changing the bend in the shoulder-in.

In both the renvers and the haunches-in the horse is bent in the direction of travel, so the outside legs step in front of the inside legs. The difference is that the hind legs move along the first track in the renvers while the front legs are moved to the inside. In the haunches-in, the front legs remain on the first track while the haunches have to yield to the inside.

The renvers can also be developed from the passade (see the section "Turn on the Haunches and Passade"). At the end of the passade, the horse is in a renvers position for a stride or two and the rider is able to keep the shoulders on the second track, and to continue with the old bend after the change of direction. This means that as soon as the horse has reached the renvers position in the passage, you should let him continue forwards and sideways along the wall in this position.

The sequence shoulder-in – passade – renvers is an old, very useful combination of movements (see illustration) which is practised at the Spanish Riding School. It can be ridden in all three gaits. In the trot and canter the degree of collection is very high, requiring a very advanced horse.

One can also continue in renvers along the long side after a half-pass. With horses who do not cross enough with the outside hind leg in the half-pass, the renvers serves to flex the inside hind leg more so the outside hind leg can cross over better.

The sequence shoulder-in – passade – renvers can be ridden in all three gaits.

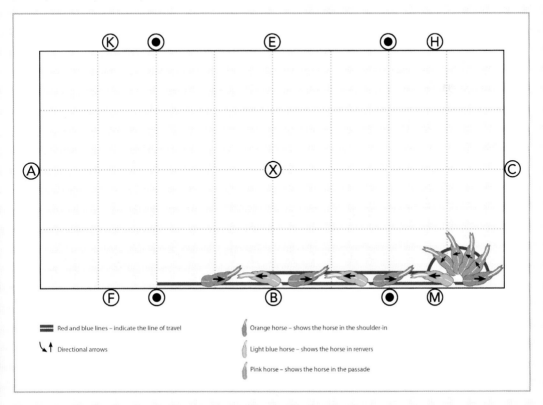

Red and blue lines – indicate the line of travel

Directional arrows

Orange horse – shows the horse in the shoulder-in

Light blue horse – shows the horse in renvers

Pink horse – shows the horse in the passage

The renvers aids correspond to those in haunches-in. The advantage of the renvers over the haunches-in is that the wall helps in framing the inside hind leg.

MISTAKES AND CORRECTIONS

Occasionally, a horse does not stay on the first track but drifts to the inside. To correct this error, bend the horse with the inside rein when the inside hind leg is grounded. Immediately afterwards, apply pressure with the outside rein against the outside shoulder to return to the wall. The inside and outside reins may have to alternate until the horse is back on the first track. The whip can be applied on the outside of the rib cage or even on the shoulder to support the outside rein.

HALF-PASS

After horse and rider have gathered some experience with shoulder-in and haunches-in, they can begin practising half-passes. I almost always choose the line from the middle of the short side to the middle of the long side for the first half-passes, but you can also ride a 10m half volte from the wall to the centre line (for instance from E or B to X) and return to the wall in a half-pass. A good preparatory exercise is to ask the horse to perform a shoulder-in during the first half of the long side until E/B, as this engages the inside hind leg. The quality of the half-pass depends on this engagement of the inside hind leg.

THE AIDS

The aids for the half-pass are a little more complex, especially during the transition from the single track to the lateral movement. To begin a half-pass, turn from the centre line on to a diagonal line as if you wanted to return to the long side on a single track. The inside hand ensures that the croup does not deviate from the line of travel to the inside too far or too early, which can happen especially with advanced horses who start to anticipate what is coming next. During the turn, you step next to the outside hind leg and raise the inside rein in a circular movement over the croup to the outside, while the outside hand applies gentle pressure against the outside hip. As soon as the inside hand reaches its destination, it takes over the lateral driving function. The outside hand guides the shoulder. The outside shoulder should follow a yielding outside rein by turning to the inside, thereby reducing the angle of the horse's body to the line of travel. Shortening the outside rein increases the angle.

If you walk next to the inside hind leg on a single track, there is an additional step. First, pass the outside hand over the croup to the outside, while changing your position by stepping next to the outside hind leg. As soon as you have crossed the line of the tail to the outside, bring your inside hand to the outside as well.

Be careful! Many horses connect their position in the arena with certain movements and produce them on autopilot. To

Lipizzaner stallion Maestoso II Shama II in the trot half-pass. (Photo: Shana Ritter)

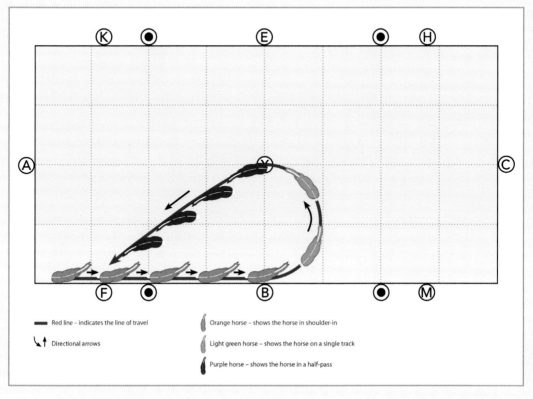

Shoulder-in-half volte from B to X-half-pass back to the wall.

*The work becomes signifi-
cantly easier when the horse
has learned to respond to a
light pressure of a finger
against the side of the hip
by sidestepping.*

prevent the horse from starting the half-pass automatically as soon as you turn down the centre line, change the rein across the length of the arena from time to time by going down the centre line on a single track.

HALF-PASS ACROSS THE LONG DIAGONAL

Now the time has come to begin half-passes on the long diagonal (M-X-K, F-X-H).

Voltes on the long side, as well as going across the width of the arena from one long side to the other, serve as preparatory exercises. This is because half-passes must be started by turning the horse's shoulder. Pretend at first you merely want to go along the diagonal. The moment the croup leaves the wall, step next to the outside hind leg, bring the inside rein across the back next

Lipizzaner stallion Maestoso II Shama II at the beginning of a trot half-pass. The moment the croup leaves the wall, the rider steps next to the outside hind leg, brings the inside rein across the back and starts the half-pass. (Photo: Mader)

to the outside hip, as described above, and start the half-pass.

MISTAKES AND CORRECTIONS

It is extremely important for diagonals and half-passes to be truly ridden as straight lines, and that the horse arrives exactly at the intended destination. Half-passes must be ridden in both directions at the same angle of the line of travel to the long side and the same angle of the horse's body to the line of travel.

The most common mistake is that the horse moves too far sideways and not forwards enough. Some horses simply drift sideways, and the rider is unable to maintain the line of travel. The horse does not arrive at the targeted destination point, but arrives at the side of the arena much too early. In these cases, the inside hind leg is not stepping sufficiently forward underneath the load and is consequently not flexing enough. The half-pass becomes gymnastically worthless.

The correction is to step behind the horse and bring the inside rein back to the inside, if necessary, in order to be able to catch the inside hind leg. The whip drives forwards on the inside, and the outside rein is either placed on top of the middle of the croup or against the point of the outside hip.

In addition, the adjustments in the aids can be supplemented by certain exercises (see the sidebar on the following page).

Improve the Half-Pass

• Interrupt the half-pass by a few strides of shoulder-in in the same direction. This brings the inside hind leg more underneath the body again.
Half-pass left to the quarter line – shoulder-in left along the quarter line, parallel to the long side – half-pass left to the centre line – shoulder-in left along the centre line, parallel to the

long side – half-pass left to the second quarter line, etc., until you reach the end of the arena.
(See drawing below)

• Interrupt the half-pass by using voltes in the same direction. Half-pass left – volte left – half-pass left (drawing top right
The transition from the half-pass into the volte connects the inside hind better to the outside shoulder, the

Interrupt the half-pass by using shoulder-in in the same direction.

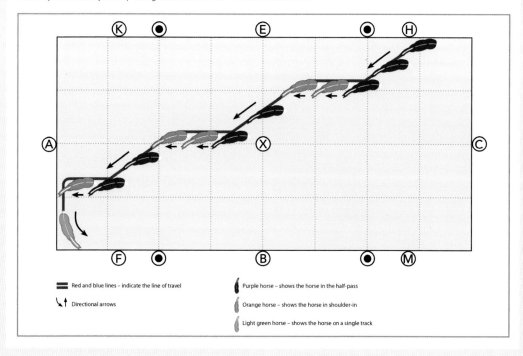

Red and blue lines – indicate the line of travel

Directional arrows

Purple horse – shows the horse in the half-pass

Orange horse – shows the horse in shoulder-in

Light green horse – shows the horse on a single track

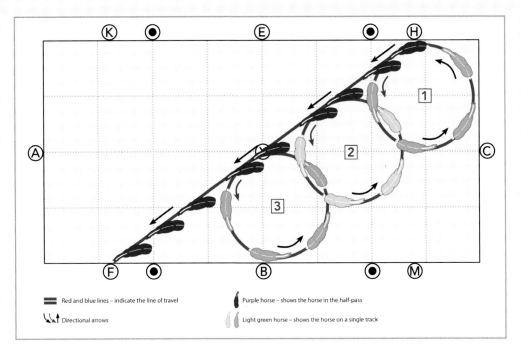

Red and blue lines – indicate the line of travel

Directional arrows

Purple horse – shows the horse in the half-pass

Light green horse – shows the horse on a single track

Interrupt the half-pass by using voltes in the same direction.

Interrupt the half-pass by using shoulder-in (see description on page 122).

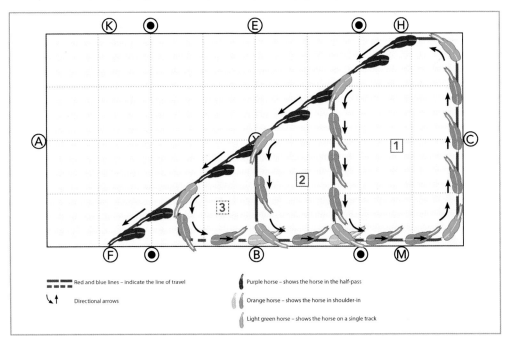

Red and blue lines – indicate the line of travel

Directional arrows

Purple horse – shows the horse in the half-pass

Orange horse – shows the horse in shoulder-in

Light green horse – shows the horse on a single track

shoulder is brought forward more, and the inside hind leg is placed more underneath the body.

Step behind the horse in the transition from half-pass to volte and send them almost directly forwards for one stride. In the next stride, turn the horse's shoulder. As soon as the horse has brought the shoulders onto the line of the volte, step slightly to the outside and ask the inside hind leg to engage if necessary, so that the lateral bend is not lost, and the horse does not fall onto their inside shoulder.

• Turn away from the diagonal in the direction of the bend and ride a

shoulder-in parallel to the short side until you reach the long side. There, turn in the same direction, ride a few strides of shoulder-in, turn through 90 degrees and continue in shoulder-in parallel to the short side until you reach the half-pass line again, and then resume the half-pass. (See drawing at the bottom of the previous page)

In this way, you can extend the diagonal at will. The inside hind leg is brought forward again and connected to the outside shoulder, so that the half-pass succeeds better after the shoulder-in.

COUNTER CHANGE OF BEND AND ZIGZAG HALF-PASSES

The next training stage involves the counter change of bend and zigzag half-passes. The counter change of bend begins either at the first letter of the long side and leads through X back to the last letter of the same long side, or the first half-pass starts in the middle of the short side, reaches the middle of the preceding long side, and ends in the middle of the opposite short

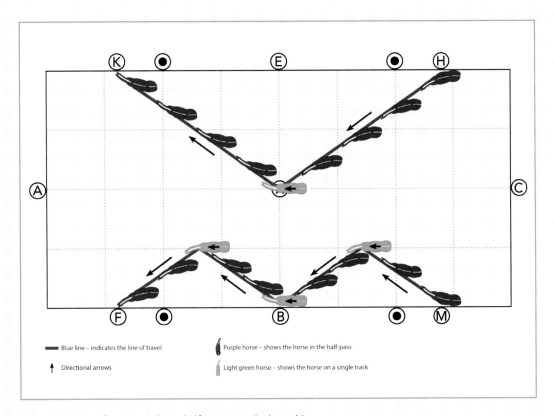

Blue line – indicates the line of travel		Purple horse – shows the horse in the half-pass
Directional arrows		Light green horse – shows the horse on a single track

Counter change of bend and zigzag half-passes on the long side.

side. Zigzag half-passes usually begin and end on the centre line. They can also be ridden between the wall and the quarter line, however.

A good preparatory exercise is the passade in the corner from the long side to the short side and back, in which the horse also has to move back and forth from side to side, while bending in the direction of travel. The most difficult moment in these exercises is the change of bend and direction. The prerequisite for a harmonious

execution of the zigzag half-pass is that the current inside hind leg stays well engaged underneath the body. Should the hindquarters drift sideways, it is almost impossible to create the new bend and to send the croup in the opposite direction.

THE AIDS

Let's take a look at the aids step by step, assuming we want to ride a transition from a half-pass left to a half-pass right. In the

The prerequisite for a harmonious execution of the zigzag half-pass is that the current inside hind leg stays well engaged underneath the body. Should the hindquarters drift sideways, it is almost impossible to create the new bend and to send the croup in the opposite direction.

from half-pass right to half-pass left, the same steps are followed in the opposite direction.

Changing from one half-pass to the other is a rather complex process that contains many opportunities for making mistakes. All the steps must be executed smoothly within three or four strides. The movements of the rider's hands are reminiscent of the flowing, round movements in Tai Chi. The rein contact must not be lost, and neither must it accidentally in-

half-pass left, the rider usually walks next to the right side of the croup. Both hands are next to the outside hind leg. During the last two strides of the half-pass, the rider walks past the horse and take their position next to the inside (left) hind leg. At the same time, the inside (left) hand is moved onto the left side of the horse. The right hand continues pushing the horse to the left. The left hand catches the horse so that the croup cannot move too far to the left. Now the right hand changes the bend. After the right bend is established, the horse's shoulders are turned to the right onto the new line. The whip can drive the right hind leg straight forwards. As soon as the horse begins the new line towards the right, the right hand is moved to the left side and the rider pushes the croup with the back of the hand towards the right. This concludes the change from left to right. During the change

Lipizzaner stallion Maestoso II Shama II in the zigzag half-pass in trot.

terfere with the horse. This is true for all transitions between lateral movements, in which the rider has to move from one side of the horse to the other. Changing sides sometimes requires lengthening the reins by three feet in order to be able to get around the croup. Then they have to be shortened again by three feet as soon as you have reached the new position. It takes a great deal of practice not to disturb the rein contact during these manoeuvres.

The rider has to slow down their own walk at certain points to let the horse gain some ground. At other times they have to move faster than the horse to catch up again. This is one of the main challenges in the lateral movements. These manoeuvres are prepared early on by letting the horse lengthen and shorten the stride and by changing positions on a single track – without disturbing the horse's rein contact, rhythm, tempo, stride length or direction. It is crucial to open or close the right door

When changing from one half-pass to the other, the rein contact must neither be lost nor interfere with the horse by accident. (Photos: Shana Ritter)

at the right moment so that the horse is able to comply with the driving aid.

Turn on the Haunches and Passade

ADVANTAGES OF THESE MOVEMENTS

Turns on the haunches and passades loosen up the shoulders and transfer the horse's body mass onto the haunches, especially the inside hind leg. They are an excellent preparation for half-passes, pirouettes and flying lead changes. The strikeoff into the canter is very successful after the passade because the inside hind leg is especially loaded and flexed in this turn. The inside hind leg of the passade becomes the outside hind leg in the canter. The outside hind leg lifts the horse into the canter. The more it advances underneath the centre of gravity, and the more it flexes underneath the load, the more uphill the horse will move in the transition and the greater the quality of the canter will be. Passades and turns on the haunches or pirouettes can be ridden in all three gaits.

HOW TO BEGIN

When the horse is starting to master the shoulder-in, you can introduce the turn on the haunches and the passade. This is usually no problem, as long as the horse steps forward willingly with the inside hind leg and stretches into the outside rein. This is why enlarging the circle and the shoulder-in are very good preparatory exercises for the turn on the haunches.

Two exercises are suitable introductions: the passade after the corner, and the turn on the haunches or passade out of the shoulder-in on the long side.

The corner works exceedingly well as a preparation, because the inside aids can send the horse in a shoulder-in related movement towards the outside rein, which then turns the horse into the passade. A horse that does not stretch into the outside rein cannot be turned. At the end of the corner, the outside rein applies a halfhalt when the outside hind leg is on the ground. Initially, it is easiest to stop briefly before starting the passade. This gives the horse enough time to think about where their feet are and where they need to go next. Later on, you can collect the horse within the gait and turn without changing gait. Passades can be ridden in all three gaits.

The line of the passade forms a quarter circle from the short side back to the previous long side, or from the long side to the short side, depending on whether the passade is ridden in the first or second corner of the short side. The horse is bent in the direction of travel. The forehand and hindquarters describe two concentric circles. The hind legs are on the smaller circle, the front legs on the larger track. The horse's spine is parallel to the radius of the turn. The corner forms the centre of the concentric circles.

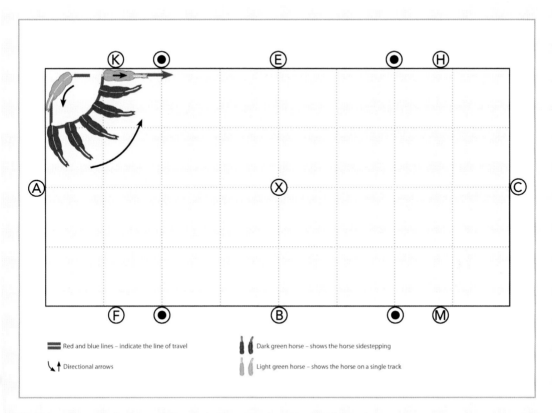

Red and blue lines – indicate the line of travel

Directional arrows

Dark green horse – shows the horse sidestepping

Light green horse – shows the horse on a single track

Passades are an excellent preparation for half-passes, pirouettes, and flying changes.

If you start the passade or turn on the haunches from a shoulder-in, the aids correspond to those of the passade in the corner described above. Usually, a 180 degree turn is performed. After the passade, either continue in renvers in the new direction, change the bend to shoulder-in, or simply continue on a single track.

WHAT IS IMPORTANT?

Make sure that the horse maintains the same distance from the corner at the beginning and the end of the exercise. Only then is the circle line round. This means that when you stop 5m after the corner and begin to turn, you should end the passade 5m after the corner on the other side. If the distance from the corner is larger after the passade than before it,

Lipizzaner stallion Maestoso II Shama II in renvers canter. This is one possible option for continuing after a passade. (Photo: Shana Ritter)

the inside hind leg did not bend enough underneath the load and the horse went through the rein instead of respecting it. If the horse is closer to the corner after the passade than before it, they came behind the aids and crept backwards.

The hips and shoulders should leave the first wall almost simultaneously and arrive almost simultaneously at the second wall. The shoulders should only be slightly in front of the haunches. If the haunches arrive before the shoulders, the horse has become crooked and the inside hind leg has moved too much sideways and not enough forwards. If the front legs arrive at the second wall a long time before the hind legs, the outside hind leg did not cross over enough, which is often caused by the inside hind leg not flexing enough under the body mass.

The turn on the haunches is a covert loop of three elements:
- *The inside hind leg steps forward*
- *The outside hind leg is brought closer*
- *The outside shoulder is turned*

THE INSIDE HIND LEG STARTS

Turns on the haunches, passades and pirouettes that begin from a halt should always be initiated by the inside hind leg taking a small step forward. The inside rein is placed on top of the middle of the croup and bends the horse to the inside. You can also press down onto the croup with it to flex the grounded hind leg. With some horses you can move the inside rein across the back to the outside. Should the horse step sideways too much with the haunches, however, bring the inside rein back onto the middle of the croup or onto the inside hip. The outside rein squeezes the rib cage laterally and turns the shoulder. Occasionally it is necessary to animate the outside hind leg with the pressure of the hand against the outside hip or with a touch of the whip to support the turn.

If necessary, the bend is improved or renewed. To correct natural crookedness, think of haunches-in on the stiffer side and of shoulder-in on the hollow side.

MISTAKES AND CORRECTIONS

The main mistakes in the passade and turn on the haunches on long reins occur when the horse turns around too quickly and too tightly or steps backwards in the turn. It may also happen that the horse loses the bend or inverts. The reason for this is that they have come behind the driving aids. The correction is to drive the inside hind leg forward so the horse turns on a slightly larger circle. If the horse throws the shoulders around, the inside rein catches them by running horizontally along the rib cage and the inside hip.

Lipizzaner stallion Maestoso II Shama II in an expressive canter. (Photo: Mader)

CANTER WORK

Prerequisites

Canter work on long reins places very high demands on horse and rider. The horse must be highly collected for the rider to be able to walk next to them. The rider must be athletic enough to keep up with a horse that is not yet very collected in the early stages, so they do not accidentally water-ski on the reins, start running or interfere in other ways to suppress the horse's thrust.

The main prerequisite for the strike-off into the canter is that the horse stretches into the outside rein with a consistent lateral bend. If this condition is not ful-filled, the horse will not canter at all, or at least not on the correct lead. The necessary bend is best achieved by riding correct corners, circles, voltes and shoulder-in. Haunches-in is a useful preparation as well, because it has a certain affinity with the canter.

This is why Gustav Steinbrecht (1808–1858), riding master and author of the well-known book "*The Gymnasium Of The Horse*", refers to a slight haunches-in position as "canter position". A slight shoulder-in position, on the other hand, is called "trot position".

Lipizzaner stallion Conversano Sorria in haunches-in canter. (Photo: Mader)

For instance, one of my horses offered canter because he did not want to step into puddles in the wet outdoor arena after it had rained. Instead, the stallion took a longer stride with his inside hind leg across a puddle, which broke up the symmetry of the footfall sequence and created a canter stride. I quickly went with him and praised him afterwards. You can see from this anecdote that these opportunities can present themselves in all kinds of situations. Afterwards, try to recreate the situation and add the canter aid. Through praise and repetition the horse learns to understand the canter aid so that, after a while, the painstaking reconstruction of the initial situation becomes unnecessary to obtain a canter depart. Following this principle, I kept heading for puddles with the abovementioned horse and applying a canter aid when he leapt across the puddle. Thus he learned very quickly to understand my intention, and the puddle

Misunderstandings

When practising spiralling in and out on the circle, shoulder-in and haunches-in at the trot the horse will occasionally offer the canter spontaneously. Always encourage the canter in this case. Do not stop the horse right away! Walk faster, keep a light rein contact, drive a little and praise the horse lavishly after the canter. Analyse which aid and which context made the horse think of the canter.

In case the horse offers the canter or a different higher level exercise without being asked, one should compliment the initiative because the horse was actively participating, in addition it has put more effort in than initially required.

became superfluous. Over the following months and years I was able to refine the canter aid to the point where I only needed to squeeze the inside rein lightly against the inside hip, followed by a release. The horse reliably took the correct lead every time I released the inside rein. The aid was invisible to onlookers.

The Strike-Off

THE AIDS

There are several different aids to choose from for the canter depart. Every horse reacts differently. Some of my horses were tuned to the yielding of the inside rein, as mentioned above. Others perform a canter transition when I touch the outside hind leg with the whip while positioning the horse to the inside. Some take the canter when I activate the inside hind leg in a slight haunches-in position. Others do it when you switch your own position to the outside, running the inside rein across the horse's back. With this method it is important to differentiate clearly between the aids for the canter, the haunches-in and the half-pass. With some horses it is helpful to increase the elevation and to lower the croup by raising the inside rein. You can activate the inside hind leg into the releasing rein, so that it takes a bigger stride and the horse starts to canter.

Of course, a horse can learn to canter from a voice command. During the early canter work, in particular, this can make training easier. Another option is to long rein with a rider in the saddle. The mounted rider asks the horse for the canter, because the horse is very familiar with this aid. At the same time, the dismounted trainer applies the canter aid with the long reins. The horse learns to associate the aids with each other and will eventually respond to the long rein aid alone.

Which option you choose depends on the horse and what they respond to best. Each of my horses chose their own canter aid.

PREPARATION

Canter transitions are difficult. They should therefore be practised frequently, along with a collected canter in lively, steady strides around the perimeter of the arena, in order to improve the pace. I spend a great deal of time cantering using the whole school while keeping the horse straight.

This highly-collected canter on long reins takes a lot of strength on the horse's part. That is why they have to take frequent breaks to catch their breath in the beginning. It is often helpful to develop the bend in the walk on a circle first, by enlarging the circle and squeezing the horse into the outside rein.

This applies especially to the horse's stiffer side, where they tend to drift in and fall onto the inside shoulder. Each time you notice this mistake, correct it by enlarging the circle for two or three strides.

PRE gelding Furia with Andreas Evertz in his first canter on long reins. The inside rein is releasing. (Photo: Shana Ritter)

Ask for the canter strike-off out of the enlarging circle when there is enough thrust and energy. If problems occur, ask for a slight haunches-in position. Some horses find trot – canter transitions easier. As is so often the case, there are no one-size-fits-all recommendations. Horse training requires a certain willingness to experiment in order to find the method that makes most sense to the individual horse. Later, canter transitions are practised on straight lines.

The Rider's Position in the Canter

In the tradition of the Spanish Riding School the rider walks next to the outside hind leg in the canter. However, this only works if the horse is very straight and does not deviate to the inside with his croup. It is much easier to walk next to the inside hind leg, because the rider can frame the inside hind leg with their own body. The outside hand

A good exercise is the combination of turns on the haunches and canter transitions. For instance, canter on the left lead from the walk, then ask for a downward transition to the walk at some point. Change rein through a turn on the haunches and then ask for the right lead canter, etc. The turn on the haunches will improve the canter by increasing the degree of collection. The canter will improve the turn on the haunches by infusing the walk with more energy. This can be repeated several times.

Lipizzaner stallion Conversano Sorria in the canter. The rider can frame the inside hind leg better through their own body by walking next to it. (Photo: Mader)

is placed on top of the croup. The inside hand stays next to the inside hip. Alternatively, the outside rein can be run across the middle of the back, so both hands are next to the inside hip. Once the horse is straighter, you can walk directly behind, and the very advanced horse can be guided from the outside without getting crooked.

MISTAKES AND CORRECTIONS

In addition to falling in with the croup, the other common mistake that happens in the canter on long reins is that the horse will gradually push the croup up more and more, while carrying the head lower and lower, which puts them more onto the forehand. This is not always easy to correct on long reins, because the rider does not have their own body weight available as an aid. Sometimes it is possible to raise the entire forehand by applying a backwards -upwards squeeze with the inside rein during the first beat of the canter stride, when the withers are rising and the outside hind leg is on the ground. This will be successful only if the horse is lifting their shoulders and withers as well. If the withers sink and only the poll rises, it is more damaging than helpful. In most cases, the main correction will have to be done under saddle.

Flying Changes

When the horse has learned the canter aid it usually does not take long before they can begin working on canter half-passes and flying changes, because the horse has been well prepared by the previous training.

THE AIDS

For the first flying change on long reins, the transition from a canter half-pass to a straight line lends itself best. Make it easy for the horse by choosing the half-pass from the middle of the short side to the middle of the long side. The aids for the canter half-pass are almost identical to the aids for the trot half-pass. At the end of the half-pass, the bend is changed. The (old) inside hand is moved to the (old) inner side to catch the croup, while the (old) outside hand creates the new bend. After changing the bend, the new inside hand is moved across the back to the outside to open the door for the croup towards the new inside. The new outside rein half-halts once or

It is crucial for a successful flying change that the horse is able to change bend at any time, to shift their weight from one side to the other at any time, and to move the croup left or right at any time.

Lipizzaner stallion Maestoso II Shama II. The canter half-pass is especially well suited as a preparation for the flying change. (Photo: Shana Ritter)

Lipizzaner stallion Maestoso II Shama II. When the horse has understood the flying change, you can practise turning away from the long side in the canter and changing leads when crossing the centre line.
(Photo: Mader)

twice into the hind leg on the same side to keep it grounded a moment longer. Immediately afterwards, the new inside hand squeezes the croup in the new direction from the outside. This hand also allows the new inside hind leg to step more forwards. The pressure against the croup from the outside triggers the flying change.

Changing the bend and half-halting on the new outside rein serve as preparation because the flying change is an automatic response to the lateral pressure of the old outside rein against the rib cage, followed by a slight squeeze of the new outside hand against the hip.

Specifically, the aids for the canter half-pass right followed by a flying change from right to left are as follows. During the half-pass right, the rider walks next to the left hind leg. The right rein runs across the back to the left hip. Both hands are next to the left hip. Should the croup move too far sideways, the inside hand is placed on top of the croup. Approaching the wall at the end of the half-pass, the rider moves behind the horse and brings their right hand to the right side, next to the horse's right hip. The left hand squeezes against the left hip and changes the bend, while the right hand catches the right hip to prevent the horse from getting crooked. The rider then steps next to the right hind leg, brings their left hand across the croup next to the right hip, and squeezes the back of the hand against the horse's right hip so the horse changes leads. The right rein half-halts against the right hind leg just before the change.

CONTINUING WORK

In order to prevent the horse from changing leads on their own without waiting for the aid, it is necessary to continue in counter-canter regularly after the half-pass. The flying change is then ridden later on the long side, on the short side, or even on the following long side. The horse should not know in advance where the flying change will be asked for. Corners in counter-canter are an excellent tool for flexing the inside hind leg. Sometimes I continue on the long side in renvers after the half-pass, which flexes the inside hind leg more. The renvers also benefits future half-passes.

Counter changes of bend and zigzag half-passes are practised in the canter as well as in the trot. The main challenge for

the rider is the smooth, harmonious change of their own position and the adjustment of the reins, without losing contact and without interrupting the gait. Once the horse and rider have mastered zigzag half-passes in the walk and trot, the canter will not present any major problems.

Once the horse has understood the aids for the flying changes they should be practised on a variety of lines and in a variety of locations in the arena. For instance, ride serpentines from one long side to the other, change out of the circle or through the circle, and practise flying changes on straight lines as well.

CONTINUING EXERCISES

First, turn away from the long side and ride parallel to the short side until you reach the opposite long side. The horse should be familiar with this exercise at the walk and trot. The flying change is performed when crossing the centre line. It is important that the horse is easy to turn with the outside aids and that they are soft and yielding on the inside aids. The bend is changed between the quarter line and the centre line. The rider steps a little more towards the old inner side, brings both reins to this side and asks for the flying change by pushing the croup slightly in the new direction when crossing the centre line. You can bring the old inside rein to the inside first. The (old) outside rein creates the new bend and enlarges the horse slightly into the old inside rein, which catches the horse. The new inside rein is now moved to the new outside as well, and the croup is pushed slightly in the new direction. With trained horses, it is often enough to change the bend and step to the new outer side. Yielding with the new inside rein after changing bend can trigger the flying change. Many of the aids I describe for the early stages will become smaller and more refined over time until they are invisible.

FLYING CHANGES ON CURVED LINES

The turns I described in the last chapter can easily be expanded into a three- or four-loop serpentine by riding semi-circles that are connected by straight lines running parallel to the short side of the arena. The serpentine loops touch the long side only for one stride, otherwise the loops would no longer be round. A variation of the same theme is the serpentine with corners,

Lipizzaner stallion Maestoso II Shama II. When the single flying change is dependable, you can begin to practise multiple flying changes on the long side or on the diagonal. (Photo: Mader)

where you continue down the long side for a few strides before turning as you would through a corner.

Flying changes when changing out of the circle or through the circle are closely related to the flying changes in the serpentine. They must be executed in a stride where the horse's body is parallel to the long side or the short side. In flying changes on curved lines, it is important the horse does not throw themselves into the turn with the inside shoulder nor turns too tightly. Given there is no aid on the new inner side, it is difficult to catch the horse if they drift to the inside with the shoulder or hip. With horses who tend to get crooked here, it is better to walk behind the croup and to run the new inside rein on top of the inner side of the croup, instead of bringing it all the way to the outside. Then you can step in faster when something goes wrong.

FLYING CHANGES ON STRAIGHT LINES AND TEMPO CHANGES

Finally, flying changes should be practised on straight lines as well. The long side offers the advantage of giving the horse a degree of support. On the diagonals, the centre line and the quarter lines, the rider must frame the horse with just the two reins. The aids are very similar to those described above. Straightness is easiest to achieve by walking behind the horse. In preparation for the flying change, frame the croup on both sides with the reins. Then bend the horse towards the outside with the outside rein

and squeeze their rib cage and hip against the inside rein so that they stretch into it. Place the outside rein on top of the middle of the croup and ask the horse to change leads with a slight pressure of the inside rein against the side of the hip. Afterwards, the new inside rein is placed against the inner side of the croup again.

This method allows you to train a series of changes by asking for a flying change at the beginning and end of a long side. When this succeeds, take the diagonal and ask for a flying change at the beginning, in the middle, and at the end of the diagonal, etc. In this way, the distances between the individual flying changes gradually become smaller. During this training stage you can tune the horse so each hand stays on its side of the croup, so the aid for the flying change consists merely of changing the bend and squeezing the old inside hand gently against the hip.

Counter-Canter

I practise the counter-canter on long reins generally after the horse has learned the flying change. It is usually not difficult to prevent the lead change with a horse who is familiar with it, but once they have become used to continuing in the counter-canter it is often difficult to teach the flying change. Once the horse has mastered the flying change, one should not always let them change leads immediately after a half-pass or a pirouette, because this could take on a life of its own and the

Lipizzaner stallion Conversano Sorria with Shana Ritter in the counter-canter. (Photo: Mader)

horse might change without listening to the aids.

Keeping the horse in the counter-canter is relatively easy. The outside rein remains connected to the outside of the rib cage and the horse's hip. The inside rein either rests on top of the croup or runs across the middle of the back so that the inside hand is also next to the outside hip. The inside rein maintains the bend. The outside hind leg can be activated if necessary. If the rider walks next to the outside hind leg, their body position can prevent the flying change.

The counter-canter in renvers position is a good tool for increasing the degree of collection and preparing beautiful flying changes. The inside rein can flex the inside hind leg effectively, especially if it runs along the centre of the croup. The outside hind leg does not step as far under in the canter as the inside hind leg. Consequently, it does not have to flex as much. This is why the horse perceives the flying change as a relief after the renvers. The counter-canter can be obtained in a variety of ways. The easiest method is to change rein across the diagonal or to change out of the circle. The counter-canter can be made into the true lead again by riding a half pirouette. You just have to select a location for the pirouette with a minimum of one horse's length distance from the arena wall. The counter-canter is thus also a great preparation for pirouettes.

Pirouettes

The canter pirouette may be the most difficult movement on long reins, because the guidance of the horse is more complicated than with most other movements. It is crucial to turn the horse stride by stride without losing the canter rhythm, the tempo, the balance, the collection or the bend. The rider must be able to determine precisely how quickly the horse turns and how large the turn is supposed to be, and

Lipizzaner stallion Maestoso II Shama II in the canter pirouette. (Photo: Shana Ritter)

must also be able to end the turn at any time by either riding straight ahead or beginning a half-pass. These are some of the challenges. This is not so easy under saddle, although the mounted rider has weight and leg aids at their disposal. On long reins, you have to make do with fewer available aids.

THE PREPARATION

Preparatory exercises for pirouettes are the lateral movements in all three gaits, walk pirouettes, passades around the corner, spiralling in on the circle, haunches-in on the circle and the counter-canter.

Dressage trainer Louis Seeger (1798–1865) gave us an important insight into successful pirouettes when he wrote: "Before starting any turn, you must have gained complete control over the outside hind leg, if you want to execute a tight turn on the inside hind leg; and this rule applies in general, relative to the tightness of the turn and the horse's dexterity." This means

The quality of all turns, from the 20m circle to the pirouette, depends on how well the rider is able to load and flex the outside hind leg.

the outside hind leg has to be well engaged under the body in order to be able to lift the forehand in every canter stride.

Control over the outside hind leg is achieved, for instance, through a plié (shoulder-in at the canter), because this exercise brings the horse into the outside rein and flexes the outside hind leg under the body mass. Haunches-in, renvers and half-pass are also good preparatory exercises, because they bring the outside hind leg more under the body.

In the counter-canter on the circle, the outside hind leg has the smallest track and therefore is the most weighted and flexed. This is why canter pirouettes from the counter-canter on the open circle side often turn out especially well.

Stopping the horse into the outside hind leg from the trot before a corner or any turn is another excellent preparatory exercise that can be practised early on, long before the horse is ready to attempt canter pirouettes. When you resume the trot afterwards, the horse will take the corner with improved balance and bend. This improvement in the corners will make itself felt in the pirouettes later on. Conversely, a horse that goes through corners with poor posture and without lateral bend will not be able to perform good pirouettes.

THE ROAD TO PIROUETTES

Photo series on right: Lipizzaner stallion Maestoso II Shama II in the canter pirouette.

(Photos: Shana Ritter)

The outside rein turns the outside shoulder, while the inside rein bends the horse and lifts the inside shoulder. Occasionally it is necessary to drive when the inside hind leg lifts off, so the horse does not break gait. In the pirouette it is especially important to release a little in every canter stride to avoid throwing the horse around and putting them on the forehand.

SPIRALLING ON THE CIRCLE

There are several possible ways to train pirouettes. One of them is by spiralling in on the circle. Spiral in with a slight haunches-in position at the walk and trot a few times. Spiralling out is done in a shoulder-in position. The first few times, spiral in only to a volte with a circumference of 12 strides of the inside hind leg. Once the horse can spiral in and out smoothly, diminish the radius further by increasing the haunches-in position and transitioning into a passage. This will lead you from a 20 m circle through the volte and the passade to the pirouette.

CANTER TRANSITIONS WITHIN THE WALK PIROUETTE

Another path, which is well suited to hot horses, is the canter transition within a walk pirouette. The best location for this is the corner. You only have to ensure you keep a minimum of one horse's length from both the short and the long side, so the horse has enough space for the turn.

Leg yield diagonally away from the long side, so you arrive on the third or fourth track one or two horse's lengths before the short side. Start a walk pirouette and apply the canter aid at the moment when the horse's shoulder approaches the short side, so both arena walls offer a visual frame. After a few canter strides in the pirouette, leave the exercise by either cantering straight ahead parallel to the short side (counter-canter) or parallel to the long side (true lead). Alternatively, you can repeat the transitions between walk and canter several times within the pirouette. I prefer the first version, because it preserves the forward urge more. However, if you have a horse that gets hot in the pirouette and throws himself around, you can correct it by repeatedly transitioning down to walk and striking off again at the canter.

The same exercise can be repeated in the canter later on. Begin in counter-canter in a renvers position. Before the second corner of the long side, ride a plié to the third or fourth track and perform the pirouette into the corner.

HALF-PASS TO PIROUETTE

A third possibility is to begin the pirouette from a half-pass. To make the work easier for the horse you could ride a half-pass from the middle of the short side to the middle of the long side. The first few times, ask for a passade just before reaching the long side and return on the long side,

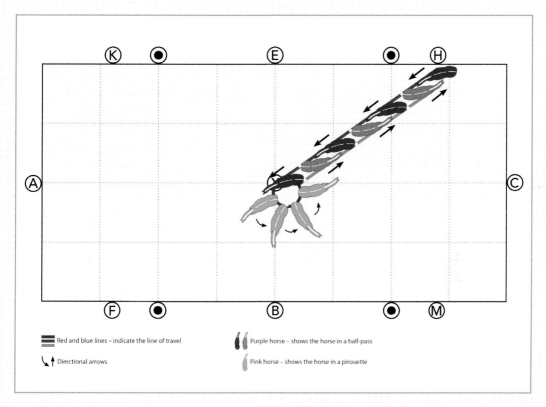

Red and blue lines – indicate the line of travel

Directional arrows

Purple horse – shows the horse in a half-pass

Pink horse – shows the horse in a pirouette

Developing the pirouette from a half-pass is one of many possibilities of training this movement.

resuming the exercise from the beginning. This can be practised at the walk and trot a few times before attempting it at the canter. The next stage in the canter con-sists of performing a half pirouette and returning in a half-pass on the same line to the letter where you started. If you started a half-pass right from C to E, you begin your half pirouette right one or two horse's lengths before E, and return in half-pass right to C. At C you can track right, to keep things simple. Afterwards, you could con-tinue by half-passing from M to X, adding another half pirouette at X and half-passing back to M. At M you have a choice of riding another pirouette, continuing in counter-canter or asking for a flying change.

THE AIDS

The best rider position is behind the horse or next to the outside hind leg. If you are too far to the outside, the horse may throw

One possible way to train pirouettes is to begin out of a half-pass. (Photo: Shana Ritter)

themselves around. If you stay more cen-tred behind the horse you can catch them with the inside rein, if necessary.

I typically run the inside rein along the centre of the croup or slightly off to the outside in order to open the door for the inside hind leg. In the first beat of the canter stride, when the withers rise, a light elevating aid of the outside rein can prevent the horse from coming too low in front and falling onto the forehand. The inside rein releases at this moment, in order to avoid suppressing the impulsion of the hind legs. In the second beat, when the main diagonal is on the ground, and during the third beat, when the inside front leg is on the ground, the inside rein can flex the inside hind leg with a half-halt or guide the shoulder towards the inside. The outside rein releases slightly at the same time, so the canter stride is preserved.

MISTAKES AND CORRECTIONS

There are several mistakes that occur frequently in canter pirouettes.

- If the horse breaks gait, the reason is usually that the rider was overusing the reins and did not release soon enough. Practise the coordination of your rein aids. Unfortunately, there is no margin for error in your timing and coordination in the pirouettes.

- If the horse throws their forehand around too quickly, the croup usually rises as well. Restore a high quality uphill canter on a straight line or on a 20m circle. This type of mistake can be corrected within the movement itself only if you catch it immediately. Canter work in general and pirouettes in particular benefit a great deal from supportive, complementary work under saddle.

Although the piaffe is an haute école movement, it can be taught to horses from Second Level and higher. (Photo: Shana Ritter)

HAUTE ECOLE

Piaffe

Piaffe, passage and the airs above the ground are part of haute école. In canter work, it is the lateral movements and the pirouettes that are traditionally counted as belonging to haute école. The preparatory work for these movements begins much earlier, however, with the correct execution of corners and lateral movements at the walk and trot. Piaffe training can begin as early as Second Level. In the widest sense all movements that make the horse more supple and more mobile in all directions serve as preparations for the piaffe. Quick reactions are also indispensable.

Only a horse that responds to an aid within the same second can become supple and lively enough to piaffe.

One could say that the quintessence of the piaffe lies in redirecting the thrust of the hind legs from a horizontal direction into a vertical direction. This requires a high degree of mobility and suppleness of the haunches, laterally as well as vertically. Consequently, you cannot obtain a piaffe by holding in front and driving behind, because these contradictory "aids" would block the horse and make them insecure by making a demand and simultaneously preventing its execution.

The quintessence of the piaffe lies in redirecting the thrust of the hind legs from a horizontal direction into a vertical direction. This requires a high degree of mobility and suppleness of the haunches, laterally as well as vertically.

THE PREPARATION

The aforementioned mobility of the horse is created and maintained by exercises that can be classified into two broad categories:
• Lateral mobilisation
• Vertical mobilisation

LATERAL MOBILISATION

Lateral mobilisation is prepared by bending in motion, i.e. by riding curved lines,

Lipizzaner stallion Maestoso II Shama II in the piaffe. (Photo: Shana Ritter)

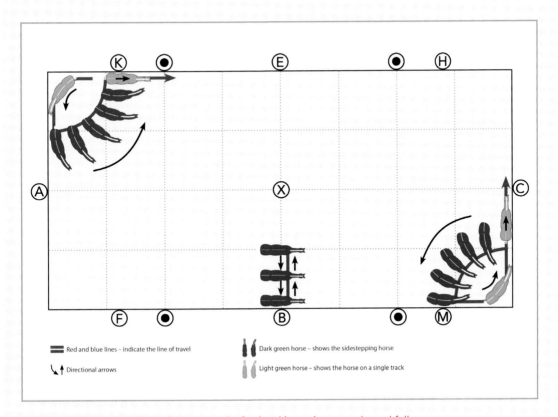

Red and blue lines – indicate the line of travel

Directional arrows

Dark green horse – shows the sidestepping horse

Light green horse – shows the horse on a single track

Lateral mobilisation is perfected by turns on the forehand in motion, passades and full-passes.

and it is perfected through lateral movements, turns on the forehand in motion, passades and full-passes. Exercises that bring both hind legs underneath the body in quick succession are especially valuable.

Here is a brief list of the various possibilities:

- Lateral movements and series of lateral movements (shoulder-in – haunches-in; shoulder – in – renvers; counter shoulder-in– haunches-in; counter shoulder-in –renvers; counter shoulder-in – haunches-in – shoulder-in – renvers; zigzag half-passes, etc.)

- Full-pass back and forth in both directions, where the horse only takes between one and three steps in each direction, and the transitions from one side to the other are performed smoothly without stopping. It is easiest for the horse to bend against the direction of travel, so that the bend changes with each change of direction.

- Turns on the forehand in motion left and right, also with only three strides in each direction before reversing. Try to eliminate the halt before each change of direction by reducing it gradually over time. The horse is bent against the direction of travel. This is the principle behind the work between pillars.

- Passades left and right, for instance right after the corner, from the long side to the short side and back. The same rules apply as in the turns on the forehand in motion. By contrast, the horse is always bent in the direction of travel in passades and pirouettes.

VERTICAL MOBILISATION

Vertical mobilisation is achieved mainly by connecting the horse's legs to the ground and through transitions. In the widest sense, this work begins with the young horse and gradually leads to the piaffe.

Here is a list of exercises for vertical mobilisation:
- Transitions: walk – halt – walk
- Transitions: walk – trot – walk
- Transitions: trot – halt – trot, shortening the duration of the halt over time
- Transitions: halt – trot – halt, reducing the number of trot strides over time
- Connecting the legs to the ground in the so-called "piaffe walk". This refers to the most collected walk the horse is capable of. Each leg is weighted individually through a rein aid (under saddle, stirrup stepping is used in addition) and the horse is asked to take livelier steps afterwards. Hotter horses diagonalise their

walk very quickly in this way, resulting in the first half steps very soon.
- Rein-back with transitions: walk – rein-back – walk (Schaukel), and direct transitions to trot from the rein-back without stopping.

In downward transitions, it is especially effective to "talk to" all four legs and to ride the transition to the walk or halt into each leg, so that all four legs let the aids go through. Under saddle, this is done with a combination of stirrup stepping and rein aids. On long reins the stirrup aid is not available, of course. This builds on the exercises I have described in the sections on holding the reins and the transitions. When the transitions flow well on a single track, it is advantageous to practise them in lateral movements as well.

ROADS TO THE PIAFFE

All the exercises that improve lateral and vertical mobility are preparations for the piaffe, as well as possible roads to the piaffe.

Most trainers have their own preferences, and every horse responds differently to the exercises. You will need to experiment a little to find the method that works best for you and for the horse you are training. Talented horses often offer half steps very early on, showing the trainer the way. Some methods work best under saddle. Others can be done in hand, in between the pillars, or on long reins. Initially, you have to be content with very few steps –

PRE stallion Mulan in the piaffe in-hand. (Photo: Mader)

and praise the horse for each promising attempt.

"If very talented horses offer piaffe steps on the first, second, or third day already, horses with mediocre talent will arrive at this point after four to six weeks, others after several months or even a year."

(B. H. von Holleuffer, 1896)

Piaffe training is very artistic. On one hand, you must have an idea of the finished product, but on the other hand you must not expect the horse to be able to produce perfect piaffe steps right away. The trainer must have a feel for which steps lead to the next level and which ones will not. While horses are learning the piaffe, they experiment a great deal with their posture and footfall, which produces some very interesting movements. It is often a little like panning for gold. The nuggets are hidden among a great deal of sand, which has to be filtered out and removed. You keep only the nuggets.

Along the same lines, the horse will offer a great many different movements during the early stages of piaffe training, but not all of them lead somewhere. The trainer should allow the horse to experiment with their body. The rider must help the horse to find the optimal balance, immediately praise them for attempts that lead in the right direction and ignore the others.

KEEP YOUR DISTANCE

It is extremely important that the horse starts to move rather vigorously from a very light aid. This is best practised in-hand or on long reins at a greater distance from the horse. This allows you to observe the horse better, and it keeps you out of reach of the hind legs. During this phase of training you will sometimes trigger small explosions, during which the horse might kick out.

Friesian stallion Richold in the piaffe. When creating more movement in the hindquarters, it is recommended to stay out of reach of the hind legs. (Photo: Shana Ritter)

It is therefore recommended to switch the long reins for a lunge line (see section "The Horse's Equipment"). During the early stages of piaffe training it is generally advantageous to walk either next to the horse's shoulder or at a greater distance behind the inside hind leg. Once the horse understands the movement, you can return to your old position on long reins, either directly behind the horse or slightly off to one side. When you are close enough to touch the horse, you can apply a downward pressure from above onto the croup with your hand or rein. Overall, you have to be careful to keep the rein contact very light in order not to interfere with the activity of the haunches.

WHIP AIDS AND WHERE TO TOUCH

The whip can be used successfully in a variety of places. However, some areas are difficult to reach from behind the horse. They are more easily accessible from the side. Generally speaking, the horse will flex the joint more that is located directly above the place that the trainer touches with the whip.

So, if you touch the canon bone with the whip, the hock will flex more in the air and the hoof is raised higher. If you touch the back of the femur, below the hip, the hip joint will flex more and the hoof will step more forwards - upwards. This often leads to a lowering and tucking of the pelvis. If you touch above the hock, the stifle will open more and the hind leg will advance more.

Touching the top of the croup causes the hindquarters to become more active overall. But be careful, this is the point where horses are most likely to respond by kicking out. Some trainers avoid touching the top of the croup altogether because some horses lift their croup in response. Often the horse will push up the croup and kick out first, but afterwards the hind legs move much more freely. This helps especially with horses who overload their hind legs, thus stifling the fluidity of the movement. Kicking out has a liberating effect in these cases.

MISTAKES AND CORRECTIONS

- Piaffe balancée: This incorrect piaffe, in which either the haunches or the shoulders sway back and forth, is usually caused by the rider trying to ask the horse to piaffe on the spot, without allowing the horse to advance, too early. In the beginning, especially, it is important that the horse advances at least half a hoof's breadth with each step in order to avoid tightness in the back and hindquarters. A piaffe on the spot cannot be expected until much later. When the horse sways with the forehand under saddle, you can push the right front leg towards the left when it is in the air, using the right knee. When the left front leg is in the air, your left knee and rein can move it towards the right. If it is the hindquarters that sway back and forth, you can open the right rein and apply the right calf when the right hind leg is lifting off. When the left hind leg is in the air, the left rein and calf can move it back under the body. On long reins, you don't have this option, of course. Here you can try to end the swaying by using a shoulder-in or renvers position.

- Four-beat piaffe: Some horses find it difficult to diagonalise their steps. They piaffe in four beats. Sometimes it is only one diagonal pair that does not touch down together, sometimes both. If it is only one diagonal pair that is not well coordinated, you can keep the front leg on the ground a little longer, while asking the diagonal hind leg to lift off faster with a driving aid. Under saddle you can also apply stirrup pressure. Several passades right and left without stopping between can help the horse to coordinate their legs. Another option is to piaffe in lateral movements. In the past it was not uncommon to piaffe in all lateral movements. Shoulder-in and renvers are especially useful in this respect.

- Front legs too far under the body: Some horses push the body mass too far forward so that the front legs are no longer vertical but too far back under the body. Elevate the horse a little more in front and let them advance slightly with each step. Conversely, a rein-back aid during the piaffe will flex the grounded hind leg and elevate the forehand more, which should also return the front legs to the vertical.

- Overloaded hind legs: Other horses shift the weight so far back that the front legs touch down too far forwards, deviating from the vertical towards the front. This overloads the hind legs, the back gets tense and the footfall sequence of the hind legs often becomes impure. In this case, you can lower the neck and make it rounder to relieve the hindquarters. Letting the horse advance a little more with each stride will also generally help.

COUNTER BALANCING WORK

An unwanted side effect of high collection in piaffe and passage is that the horse's abdominal muscles and hips can become laterally tight and braced. This makes it necessary to alternate the piaffe and passage work with lateral movements, voltes and figures of eight, in order to relax these muscles. Because it is difficult to achieve an effective lateral bend on long reins, work under saddle plays an important role here. Seat, weight and legs can frame the horse better, and the mounted rider is able to feel and remove tension in the abdominal and croup muscles better than on long reins. Apart from this, the high degree of collection must be balanced by riding more forwards, because any imbalance in the workout will sooner or later lead to stiffness. However, if you ride forward in medium and extended gaits for too long, suppleness and relaxation will suffer as much as if you ride only highly collected gaits.

PRE stallion Amigo with Andreas Evertz. Work in high collection has to be balanced with riding forwards, as well as with lateral movements and curved lines. (Photo: Shana Ritter)

Passage

There are several possible ways in which the passage can be approached. The most effective method is a path that combines work in-hand, training under saddle and long reining, just as in the piaffe. Most trainers agree that the passage should be taught to the horse after the piaffe, because many horses have trouble learning the piaffe after the passage. Of course,

all rules have exceptions. There are horses whose piaffe tempo is so slow that it resembles a passage on the spot. In these cases it might be better to start with the passage. Most horses, however, have a piaffe which is closer to the trot in tempo, i.e. faster than the tempo of the passage.

> *During work in high collection, such as piaffe and passage, the horse's abdominal muscles and hips can easily become laterally tight and braced. This makes it necessary to alternate piaffe and passage work with lateral movements, voltes and figures of eight, in order to relax these muscles again.*

ROADS TO THE PASSAGE

There are three main approaches that can produce a passage:
1. Lengthening the strides in the piaffe
2. Slowing the tempo down in the trot
3. From the walk, especially the Spanish walk, by raising the shoulders

1. If the trainer decides on the first approach, the horse needs to be able to vary their stride length in the piaffe. After a few strides almost on the spot, allow the horse to go more forwards and ask the hind legs to push more. After several bigger strides, you can either shorten the strides again, or stop the horse, praise them, and begin again. This is easier to do in-hand or under saddle than on long reins. Ask the horse for livelier steps while releasing the increased energy into longer strides with your hand. The thrust should take a forwards - upwards direction, more vertical than horizontal. Once the croup muscles get stronger and the grounded hind leg is able both to push and to carry more, the horse will be able to take longer, slower, more suspended strides forwards from the piaffe.

As an alternative, you can ask the horse for very lively steps in the piaffe first. This inner fire is channelled into a powerful collected trot. Then, slow the strides down with half-halts into the outside hind leg, followed by half-halts into the inside hind leg. Slowing down a very energetic trot leads to a longer suspension phase and thus the passage. This is a combination of obtaining the passage from the piaffe and the trot.

2. If you decide to develop the passage from the trot, lateral movements are an important preparation. There is a certain relationship between the haunches-in, the half-pass and the passage, and between the shoulder-in, renvers and the piaffe. There are two methods that complement each other well. First, ask for a few strides of haunches-in on the long side, focusing on the lively engagement of the outside hind leg. Quickly return to a single track and slow down the outside hind leg with two half-halts. If necessary, apply a driving aid so the slower tempo does not result in a loss of energy, but in an increase of expressiveness. Immediately afterwards, apply two half-halts into the inside hind leg. If necessary, activate the hindquarters

Lipizzaner stallion Maestoso II Catrina in the passage. (Photo: Shana Ritter)

again. The underlying principle consists of energetically engaging the outside hind leg under the body and flexing it afterwards with the body mass.

Second, riding a half-pass also engages the outside hind leg. In contrast to the previous exercise, the half-halts are applied into the hind leg that was on the inside in the half-pass, after reaching the arena wall. In a left half-pass, it is the right hind leg that must cross. Upon arrival on the rail, the left hind leg is flexed with the half-halts and kept on the ground for a moment longer. The steeper the line of the half-pass you choose, and the sooner the horse arrives on the long side, the more the inside hind leg is flexed in the half-pass. This increases the horse's desire to push off again. The horse perceives the passage on a single track as a relief compared with the much more tiring half-pass on a steep line. The two half-halts into the outside hind leg are followed by a driving aid as well, in order to increase the vertical push. The process is repeated immediately afterwards for the inside hind leg: slow down the tempo with two half-halts, then activate with a driving aid.

3. The third possibility for training the passage is to touch the front legs so the horse lifts their shoulders more, and then to ask for a trot transition by activating the hind legs. If the horse has talent for the passage, they will push off more vertically in the trot transition, which can lead to passage-like steps. An assistant is required for this type of work; they must walk next to the horse with two whips. A relatively stiff whip is generally used for touching the front legs, while the hind legs are touched with a more flexible whip.

When long reining, the rider can help the horse understand their intentions by pressing down onto the croup muscles with the rein hand during the half-halts. The first passage steps have little in common with the finished product. As with the piaffe, it is a constant process of filtering, explaining, correcting and polishing until the finished movement develops.

A good passage requires a great deal of enthusiasm on the horse's part. Lively, spirited animals are especially well-suited to this movement. Calm personality types at least have to be able to be stimulated enough by the sequence of exercises to create the exuberance that is necessary for the passage. The same is basically true for the piaffe. The trainer must recognise the horse's talent(or lack thereof) for these movements, and take it into consideration during the work, in order not to make unrealistic demands of the horse.

MISTAKES AND CORRECTIONS

A mistake that occurs in the piaffe, as well as in the passage, is the uneven movement of the diagonal pairs of legs. The hind leg of the hollow side often takes bigger steps than the hind leg of the stiffer side. The root cause is the horse's natural crookedness. The hind leg of the stiffer side is stronger and pushes more, but it carries less. The greater thrust of this hind leg causes the hind leg of the hollow side to advance further. Because the hind leg of the hollow side is weaker it pushes less, so that the hind leg of the stiffer side touches down early and cannot engage enough, owing to the lack of support of the other hind leg. This is a fundamental problem and therefore cannot be corrected in the piaffe or passage itself. Once this deficit in the basics is removed, the horse will step evenly in the piaffe and passage as well.

The piaffe improves the canter. The passage improves the trot.

Levade

In the past, raising the front legs was called a pesade. Towards the end of the nine-

The piaffe improves the canter. (Photo: Mader)

teenth century the differentiation between levade and pesade was introduced. In a levade, the horse's body forms an angle of about 30 degrees with the ground. The haunches are deeply flexed, and the hocks almost touch the ground. In a pesade, however, the horse's body forms an angle of up to 45 degrees with the ground, and the haunches are slightly less flexed. The lower the forehand, the more the joints of the hindquarters will be flexing under the weight, and the closer the hocks are to the ground, the more strength is required and the more perfect is the execution of the movement. In a perfect levade the withers are barely higher than at the halt, but the croup is clearly lowered. The front legs should be flexed and tucked. In order to stand more securely, some horses widen

The first attempts at piaffe and passage bear little resemblance to the finished product. The trainer must allow the horse to experiment with their body, and then recognise and praise those movements that lead to the next level, while ignoring the others. In this way, the finished product develops through a process of filtering, polishing, sifting, explaining and correcting.

their stance by bringing their hocks closer together and their feet farther apart than in the piaffe.

REARING AND OTHER MISTAKES

There is a clear distinction between levade and pesade on the one hand and rearing on the other. When it is rearing, the angle between the horse's body and the ground is steeper than 45 degrees and the hind legs are completely straight. This is in reality a disobedience that has nothing to do with dressage, much less with haute école. Another typical difference is that horses generally rise slowly and carefully into the levade, whereas the rearing horse goes up quickly, abruptly and steeply.

The levade develops out of the piaffe. Sometimes you see riders ask for the levade from the halt. This should be avoided, because the horse can too easily brace the abdominal and croup muscles, and get behind the aids. The levade then devolves into rearing.

If the horse is sufficiently prepared, you can lift them with one finger into the levade. It is crucially important that the horse remains in front of the driving aids and does not suckback. In shifting the weight back onto the haunches the horse may take a step or two backwards in order to balance on two legs. This is not ideal, but it is not necessarily a grave mistake, as long as the horse is thinking forwards and can easily be prompted to go forwards again. The rider must develop the feel and

Lipizzaner stallion Maestoso II Catrina in the levade. The major difference between a levade and a rear is that the joints of the hindquarters are flexed in the levade and the front legs are tucked, whereas the haunches of a rearing horse are stiff and straight, and the front legs are usually also extended, or may even gesticulate wildly in the air. (Photo: Shana Ritter)

the experience to recognise whether a horse is taking a step back in order to find their balance or whether they are hiding behind the driving aids. In the first case, they will raise the forehand slowly and stay rather low. In the second case, they will rise more quickly and steeply.

THE ROAD TO THE LEVADE

Traditionally, the airs above the ground are taught in-hand first before adding the rider's weight. This both makes it easier for the horse and lowers the risk for the trainer. In the past, the airs above the ground were practised in the pillars as well, which is especially risky in the case of the jumps, because the horse has very little space in which to move.

During the piaffe training a horse will periodically initiate airs above the ground, which shows where their talents lie. When you increase the energy and the degree of collection in the piaffe, some horses offer a levade, while others offer the early stages of courbettes or caprioles. You should ignore the attempts at jumping in the beginning, because if you reward them too soon, the horse may use them against the rider as a defence against half-halts by jumping upwards through the rider's hands. Out-of-control courbettes can be especially unpleasant. Levades, on the other hand, are always useful, as long as the horse rises slowly and stays close to the ground, because they flex the haunches and strengthen the croup muscles.

Transitions into the levade usually happen when the horse shifts so much weight on to the haunches that a single hind leg is not strong enough to support the load by itself. The horse then puts down the other hind leg and raises the forehand. Many horses proceed very carefully, lifting a single foreleg at first, while keeping the tip of the toe of the other foreleg on the ground to secure their balance.

The first attempts are usually no more than a brief tucking of the front legs, and the horse stays close to the ground. This is perfectly fine in the beginning. As the hindquarters gain strength the horse will be able to stay in the levade longer. Resist the temptation to force the horse to keep the forehand in the air longer, because it can easily lead to paddling and waving of the front legs, which is always indicative of a loss of balance. Rearing is almost always accompanied by waving front legs. It is better to repeat the short attempts regularly and be patient, until the muscles of the hindquarters have become stronger.

AIDS

During work in-hand you can obtain the levade by raising the hand that is holding the lead rein. The wrist remains supple and the rein contact is very light, in order not to interfere with the impulsion.

On long reins, stand behind the horse in the piaffe, place your hands on top of the croup, and briefly press down with both hands while applying a light upward

Lipizzaner stallion Conversano Sorria with Shana Ritter in the levade in-hand. In the levade, the horse's body forms a 30 degree angle with the ground. (Photo: Mader)

pressure with both reins. If an assistant is available, they can use a cavesson and lead rein to ask the horse to piaffe and levade, while the trainer with the long reins also applies a levade aid. This builds a mental bridge for the horse, so that they learn to understand the long rein aid faster.

LEVADE AND MÉZAIR

The levade improves the impulsion and collection of the piaffe. It is therefore not only an haute école movement for display, but also quite a useful gymnastic tool.

If you activate the hindquarters as soon as the front legs touch down again, the horse will perform a series of quick and short levades that used to be called mézair, and that can be used as a preparation for courbettes and caprioles. However, the mézair itself will strengthen the musculature of the hindquarters and create a certain inner fire in horses that otherwise tend to be rather phlegmatic. This movement is

Lipizzaner stallion Maestoso II Shama II in the pesade. In this movement, the horse's body forms a 45 degree angle with the ground. (Photo: Mader)

nowadays often referred to as a terre-à-terre. The classical literature generally defines the terre-à-terre as canter-related haunches-in, in two beats. The front legs lift off and touch down together, and then the hind legs lift off and touch down together. The mézair, on the other hand, is a movement on a single track in two beats. These movements are similar, and differ primarily in that the mézair is ridden on straight lines, whereas the terre-à-terre is also ridden on curved lines and belongs among the haunches-in related lateral movements.

The author with the Lipizzaner stallion Conversano Sorria.
(Photo: Mader)

CONCLUSION

Don't Give Up

Long reining is at least as difficult as riding: Nobody is able to learn it within a weekend, a month, or even a year. Only those who study it intensively for many years become good at it. The work can be tiring and frustrating at times, particularly if you are unable to coordinate your hands and feet the way you imagined right away. This always reminds me of my high school English teacher who used to tell us with a grin: "It has always taken a little more effort to acquire a higher education". And that is exactly what serious riding in general and long reining in particular is all about. Egon von Neindorff told me many years ago that long reining had always been the work of the masters. One must therefore not be discouraged if the road seems long and rocky.

This kind of work is also a lot of fun and can become addictive. It trains the rider's eye and feel by correlating a feel with a visual impression, and vice versa. One of the things that make this type of work so appealing is its minimalism. The equipment is limited to the bare minimum, and the rider remains discreetly in the background, so nothing distracts the eye of the observer from the horse as the main performer. It is therefore an especially beautiful way of presenting a horse in public which audiences like very much and which the participants enjoy visibly.

APPENDIX

Literature

Becker, Horst:
Handbuch der Doppellongenarbeit,
Cadmos 2003, Chapter 5 and 6.

Dietz, Alfons:
Die klassische Bodenarbeit,
Cadmos 2000, Chapter on Der lange Zügel
– die Krone der Bodenarbeit.

Fielder, Paul:
All About Long Reining,
J.A. Allen 1999.

Giffels, Ruth:
Klassisch-barockes Reiten:
Grundlagen des Reitens, der Arbeit and
der Hand und am Langen Zügel,
Franck-Kosmos 2008, Chapter on Long
Reining on the ground.

Gunzer, Saskia/ Künzel, Nicole:
Am Langen Zügel,
WuWei 2011.

Hill, Cherry:
Longeing and Long Lining the English
and Western Horse,
Howell 1998.

Hill, Cherry:
101 Longeing and Long Lining Exercises,
English and Western, Howell 1998.

Contact

Hinrichs, Richard:
Pferde schulen an der Hand,
Franck-Kosmos 2005,
Chapters on long reining.

Karl, Philippe:
Hohe Schule mit der Doppellonge,
BLV 1990.

Loriston-Clarke, Jennie:
Lungeing and Long-Reining,
Kenilworth Press 1993.

Radtke, Stefan:
Pferde gymnastizieren mit
der Doppellonge,
Kosmos 2010.

Schuthof-Lesmeister, Ellen/Kip Mistral:
Arbeit an der Hand. Klassische Lektionen,
Müller-Rüschlikon, 2010,
Chapters on long reining.

Stanier, Sylvia:
The Art of Long Reining,
J.A. Allen 1993.

www.klassische-reitkunst.com
thomasritt@gmail.com
www.aischbachhof.com

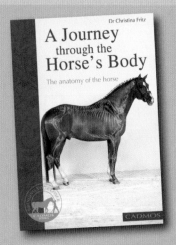
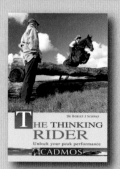
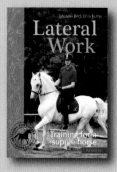
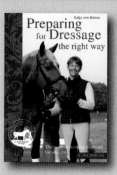
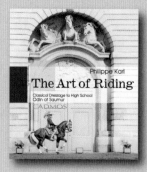